# DEDICATION

To anyone who has lost a loved one, felt alone & like there was no

light at the end of the tunnel.

There is hope.

# CHASING TIME

## MARISSA D'ANGELO

# CONTENTS

# ACKNOWLEDGMENTS

I cannot express enough thanks to everyone in my life that had continued to support me along this journey. My family and friends have supported me in remarkable ways.

Therapy has helped me find my voice again through writing and art. Thank you, Elizabeth Hlavek.

Special thanks to my Krav Maga instructor, Shannon Lord, you have helped me gain confidence both inside and out, doing what I know my father would've wanted me to do.

# CONTENT WARNING

Chasing Time is a memoir that includes diary entries that date back to World War II, therapy sessions and true accounts of events that have occurred. The story includes elements that might not be suitable for some readers. Mentions and recounts of death/illness of a parent, references to bullying, addiction and sexual assault are present in the novel. Readers who may be sensitive to these elements, please take note.

# 1

# COMMENCE

Just start at the beginning" is what they always said to me. But where? Which part? There were so many starting points to choose from. Most of the time, I stayed away from the present and things that had just happened, as childhood seemed much more memorable to me. I always felt like there was more, though. Sometimes when I would think about certain memories that I had, I would hit a brick wall and knew there were bits and pieces of the memory I must have blocked out. After years of being silent, I was finding myself at yet another therapist. If all the beginnings were so good, then why did it lead me down this path?

I was again walking into yet another office to be questioned as I awkwardly sat there. I reluctantly grabbed the handle to the door and swung it open, already feeling pressured to reopen wounds that were barely healed to begin with. The building was off to the side, a bit from everything else in town. I liked that no one else accompanied me. It meant that much less interrogating. Part of me kept pushing to go, as if there would be a sudden breakthrough at some point into my past.

When I entered, there was a directory on the immediate right that showed several different practices and their locations. I shuffled for my phone, forgetting the therapist's name. Scrolling through my calendar, I finally found it. I traced each cluster of names with my eyes until I came across one to match the name in my phone:

Cecilia Barnes — Floor 2B

I took a deep breath and checked my phone. I had two minutes to spare. One thing I hated in the world was rushing around, so I always tried to be early if I went anywhere. I headed up the steps, not wanting to wait on the sketchy looking elevator and stood before 2B. The door was shut, but there were some seats on the outside and a sound machine was plugged in. Soothing ocean waves attempted to make people forget where they were. The machine matched the one I had at home and used during the night to fall to sleep. The ocean was one place I went when life became unbearable. There was a small lounge area with a coffee table in between that held various therapeutic exercises. Psychology magazines were laid out in the center of the table and on the right side of it was a Mandala coloring book. To the left, a Zen Garden. I had a small replica of that at my office desk, but it was a Zen Litter Box that I bought for shits and giggles. When I ordered it, I was expecting it to be a regular sized Zen box, but it was instead about two by two, which I quickly uncovered after finding a tiny box in the delivery package. The Zen Garden is helpful for some, it creates a distraction that is needed much of the time. It is full of sand and includes a tool to smooth out the sand. On one side, it is a fork that creates lines, whereas the other side is a roller and smooths it out. I sat beside the Zen Garden and began smoothing out the sand, chuckling to myself as this one was missing the little cat figures mine had. I got lost in my own thoughts when I heard the muffled voices coming from the other side of the door. In a matter of seconds, the door was gently pushed open, allowing what looked like another patient to leave. A girl walked out that had to be taller than six feet with hot pink hair. It shagged over most of her pale face as she glanced at me, then quickly moved her attention back to the therapist on the other side of the door. I could only see her nose ring poking out and not much else. She wore combat boots and dark clothes. After confirming their next appointment, the loud squeaky combat boots made their way out.

"Marissa? Come on in!"

I let out a sigh and walked into her office. It was quite small and had a deep brown table with a single chair on each side. There were motivational quotes on various canvases throughout the room. As I grew more and more enamored with looking around, I noticed the therapist's handout welcoming me.

"Marissa, I am so glad you came! You can have a seat if you like. I am Cecilia, but everyone just calls me Cece." As she gestured to one of the empty chairs. She spoke in a very calm tone. When I took her hand in mine, she gave it a gentle shake as I grew startled by how cold her touch was. Her dirty blond hair was back in a bun, and she had an olive complexion with freckles sporadically about her face. Her thin nose led up to dark green eyes. She definitely looked to play the part well as a therapist since she had black dress pants on and a plain white blouse; it was all very simple, yet professional.

I sat in the chair expecting her to begin asking typical questions such as, "How do you feel?" and, "Tell me about yourself," but there was silence as she took the seat across from me. No longer was I the one making others feel awkward. This time, I was getting a dose of my own medicine. But why? I could hardly understand it. Didn't she have a job to do? We sat like that for what felt like all of eternity. I shuffled for my watch to see only twenty minutes had gone by. Cece was writing vigorously in a notebook.

I broke the silence. "What are you writing about?" I had asked.

She smiled as she looked up at me and set down her pen. "Sometimes we can't find the words or speak about things in life that happened to us. Writing about them is often much easier. I am just free writing. Anything that comes to mind, really. It doesn't have to be good memories or bad, it can be anything. You can try it if you'd like." She had a blank notebook ready to go with a jar of newly sharpened pencils and pushed them toward me.

# 2
# BEGINNINGS

There was a short time left of the session, but I wanted to write something good. I wasn't ready to dig into any bad memories quite yet. One memory kept running through my mind of my dad and me at the playground. My first school where I attended kindergarten was in a very small building by the town hall that consisted of solely the kindergarten.

This was the first day I ever attended school and Dad parked his huge pickup truck in front of the brick building that was colossal to me at the time. He had parked right in front of the entrance while I waited for him to walk around to my side, where I sat in my booster seat. He opened the door.

"Where are we going, Daddy?" I had asked.

He looked down. I didn't know why he looked so sad at the time. When he brought his face back up, it was as if he put a mask on, displaying opposite emotions from what he had just shown. "This is your first day of school! You're going to meet so many people. You'll love it!!"

"Ok daddy. We will have such a good time!" I said, not understanding he would not be attending kindergarten with me. He picked me up and placed me on the sidewalk next to his truck while he unloaded my small backpack that didn't have much in it except for a lunchbox with Lunchables. He put it over his shoulder, slammed the door shut and held my delicate hand between his thumb and pointer finger.

I looked around me and could hear laughter coming from

the playground next to the main building we were about to go into. It was September, and the leaves were already starting to change to shades of red, yellow, and orange on all the trees around us. We made it to the door. Dad didn't let go of my hand, but instead used the other to open the door and led me into the entrance. We were instantly greeted by some older lady at a desk. She had curly gray hair and thick-rimmed glasses that had fallen down to the bridge of her nose.

"Welcome to Mary L. Tracy!" the lady cheerfully said. She walked right up to my father and shook his hand without wasting a moment. Then she looked down at me and said, "Hi there! What is your name? I am Miss Shirley." She held out her hand. I wasn't sure at the time what to do with her hand, so I just looked up at my dad nervously and waved to her. She smiled in response. I guess I had responded in the right way! She had directed us to follow her, as my "classroom" would be just down the hall. As we followed her, I could hear children giggling, while in other directions of the hall, some were definitely crying. This made me feel uneasy, but at least Dad would be with me.

We arrived at the last room on the right of that hallway and Miss Shirley knocked on the door. There were two adults inside the room and the rest looked like kids like me from what I could see from the window into the room. One of the adults signaled to the other, and she started walking toward the door.

The lady was a younger teacher and might have been what I used to call a "helper." This was an important job that people had. They didn't give all the rules, but they helped everyone to follow them. I had seen this before somewhere...maybe on TV. She looked nice and was smiling like all the other adults here so far. She had dark brown hair that was back in a ponytail and had pale skin with brown eyes. She kind of reminded me of what I looked like.

The door swung open, and she pressed her back against it to hold it for us. "Hey guys! I am so glad you could make it. Are you Joseph?" she asked my dad.

"You can call me Joe! Yeah, and this is little Marissa." He gestured over to me, still holding my hand this whole time. I could feel my hand getting sweaty after being held, but I didn't wanna let go because this was a new place. For some reason, the "helper" lady took my bag from Dad and put it around her own shoulder. She then bent down to get closer to me.

"Hey there, Marissa! Welcome to Kindergarten. There are so many children here that are eager to meet you! You will have a lot of fun, you'll see!!" She took my hand and I reluctantly let go of Dad's. They must have had some form of agreement because the next thing I knew it, I was guided into the classroom with the other kids and the door was shut behind me. I went toward the window by the door that showed into the hallway and realized my dad was still on the other side. I panicked, sending my arms swinging and my legs kicking all around. Dad was supposed to come in with me to kindergarten; this wasn't the plan. What was kindergarten, anyway?

I could see Dad burst into tears on the other side and he looked as though he was going to open the door and just take me home as I agreed with at the time, but instead Miss Shirley put her arm around him and led him away from the door and out. After crying and crying for what seemed like forever, I sat there right by the door and pouted, with my arms crossed in front of my chest. The adults tried to talk to me to get me to come to "circle time," whatever that was... but all I kept saying was, "I don't." This was a common thing I said when I was being stubborn. It felt like I had been there a while, and I could hear some of the kids giggling on the carpet. Suddenly, everyone filed out the other door to go outside. I kept my arms crossed but glanced behind me and one of the "helpers" must have seen that I was curious. She walked over to me.

"Would you like to come out, Marissa?" she asked. I didn't respond. She called over to another kid. "Katie, do you want to show Marissa the playground?"

In just a few moments, a girl who was just a few inches taller than me walked over and extended her hand out. "Hi, I'm Katie. What's your name?" she asked. I didn't answer. She grew impatient. "Come on, let's go to the playground. Maybe you'll see your dad from there!" This completely won me over at the chance that I could see him or escape this doom. I didn't take Katie's hand, but walked side by side with her, trying to pretend not to notice the adults smirking as they thought they got their way. Nope, they'll see. I'll get out of here!

When we made it outside, I felt like I was in seventh heaven. The entire playground was made of wood and looked like a castle! There were many tunnels to go through and hidden parts. As soon as Katie and I got inside the fence, she said, "Quick, follow me!" and burst into a run. I tried my best to keep up with her. I ran through the entrance to the wooden playground castle and followed Katie through the tunnels and up a few stairs to reach one of the several lookout points.

"Do you see any pirates?" she said as she looked afar.

I looked out and thought I would follow along with her game. "Yes, there!!" I pointed at a random child I had never seen before.

Katie let out a scream, and I mimicked her screaming, "AHHHH!!" We ran out of the lookout tower and down a slide toward the area I had pointed to. I found the random child and said, "You're it!" running away, giggling uncontrollably. I tried to hide behind one of the tunnels but found myself still laughing.

"Marissa!!!" someone called. I looked over and saw Daddy. He looked so happy to see me having fun, but I could tell he was a little hurt because he expected to see that I missed him more. If only he could have played Pirates with us, that would have been the cherry on top! I waved to Katie and the other kids and then grabbed my bag, heading over to Dad. He scooped me up and said how proud of me he was that I made it through the day.

"You are so strong, you're stronger than me!!" I laughed because he had such big muscles that couldn't possibly be true.

I made muscles with my own arms and yelled out "URGH!" which always made him laugh. "Wait till I tell mom. We'll get some ice cream later too to celebrate! Way to go, Slim!"

I put down the pencil and couldn't help but feel a smile spread across my face. I wondered if I had been smiling the entire time I was writing this memory. I could have written it like it was in the past, but I wanted to relive the experience every time I came back to read it because it was such a powerful moment in my past.
"See you next week?" Cece asked. I nodded and headed out.

# 3

# LOUIS & MARTHA

The following week dragged by, but I kept wondering what I would write about next. There were so many stories from my childhood that came right to mind, but it was difficult to choose which I should talk about. I felt there was a deep purpose in each word I said when I wrote it down on paper. My great grandfather had dementia, and I knew I would want to keep my memories safe on something more permanent than my own mind. My job as a teacher seemed to keep my mind occupied enough each day, but it was when I had an empty schedule—which I tried to make sure never happened—that I was forced to face my own thoughts, which was scarier to me than anything. Although teaching could take hours and hours upon my normal schedule, I was always thankful in a way as it provided me with the stability and structure I needed to get me by.

That day in therapy, I focused on my Grandpa Hiyi because he was someone I spent a lot of time with and there was more to him than many people knew. I chose to come to therapy toward the end of the week so I wouldn't have work weighing on my shoulders so much and I could focus, so I drove on a Friday right after I got out. It was beautiful outside, and I regretted not spending more time outside than cooped up and writing. I walked my way toward the waiting room outside Cece's door and didn't even get a chance to sit down when the door flung open, and she welcomed me right in.

"Hey there! I am glad you could make it again, Marissa," she said with a warm smile. This time her hair was down from her bun, and she looked much more casually dressed as if she had changed and I was her last appointment of the day. It gave me a bit of comfort to see her in relaxing clothes, as it made me feel more relaxed myself. This time, I wasn't so silent. "Hey Cece. Thanks for putting me on your schedule! Last week actually helped a bit." I gave her a shy smile and walked over to where I had sat last time. I picked up the pencil and notebook that she had already put out in preparation for me, as if she knew I was going to write again. As I opened to the next page, I felt the need to address something with Cece.

"It's ok if I just write again, right? I don't know if I am ready to talk yet," I asked, nervously looking down at the paper again instead of right at her.

"Of course! This is your time. You can use it as you need. If you feel more comfortable writing, go right ahead. And at any time, you can talk to me but feel free not to as well." She walked around the table and sat on the other side as she had done before. This time, she brought out a sketchbook as opposed to a journal. I brought my focus back to my journal.

For as long as I could remember, Grandpa Hiyi was a simple, but silly, old man. He was a man of few words, but mostly actions which truly matter the most. He always kept his face clean-shaven; probably something that was drilled into him from the military; and his hair had started graying but still had some shades of black. He had kind, chocolate eyes that made you feel okay just by looking into them and very fuzzy eyebrows full of gray and black hairs. Where did I get "Grandpa Hiyi" from, you ask? Whenever he would walk around and something crazy was happening or he didn't know what to say to something, he would just say, "Aye yi yi." This was just a fitting name for him!

When I was in 5th grade, I did a report on my family and had to question him about his previous years in the war. He did not want to talk about it much, but I do know this for a fact: Grandpa was from Hungary and was only able to attend a few years of schooling at the elementary level, as he had to help his family on the farm. Back then, things were much different. When he got older, he was going to be drafted into World War II, but did not want to join under Hitler's armies and since his sister had moved to America, he said that he had lived there with her as well. Back then, there were not many ways to track people as there are nowadays. Now, anyone and everyone can know where you are at all times. It is quite scary. Anyway, Grandpa ended up coming over to America where met a woman named Martha who he fell in love with, but had to go to war because he was drafted into the military. When he had gone overseas to fight and see all the unimaginable horrors there were over there, he came back, and Martha had been waiting for him all along. She wrote him this letter on a typewriter

September 15, 1944

Dear Lou,

This letter will be one of reminiscence. I will reminisce about the wonderful time that I once had with a person who I thought was like every other fellow but who was very much unlike the rest of the fellows that I knew.

I met this young man in church. I was singing in church one beautiful Sunday morning and my eye caught a very sad, lonely face in the midst of the congregation. I immediately felt sorry for this person and wanted to ask him to join the choir because the rest of the younger people in the church belonged to this particular organization.

After church service, I went out to ask him to come down on Monday night and he said he would think about it. He didn't seem very promising, but he said, "maybe." I didn't even know the fellow's name and didn't think of asking him. There was another fellow watching me and he wanted me to go out with him that afternoon and I told him that I couldn't because I had a cousin who was coming to see me, and I didn't want to leave her alone. He always kept bothering me for dates and I think that he knew that I didn't care for him and that probably made him come around all the more.

Well, the story goes on; the bell rang as I was doing the dishes and Mother answered the door. There were two fellows down at the front door and I sometimes wonder what was in their minds. I bet mother never thought then that one of those fellows would be her future son-in-law. The two fellows came up and sat down and I was scared stiff because I knew one of them, but the other one was a complete stranger. I didn't even know his name.

Well, the one that I knew, Bert introduced the other fellow as Louis Toth and then I knew his name. They wanted to take me to a baseball game, but I guess they didn't know that they stopped playing baseball a month before, but I fooled them and played along with them in their little game.

We looked all over for a ball game, but there weren't any, so we went to a movie, and I sat between both of them. One of them kept trying to hold my hand and then the other one slumped down into his seat and enjoyed the picture, although he looked very bored.

I took the fellows home after we went to church that night and we ate hot dogs and baked beans at my house and talked for a while. We were supposed to attend a meeting at a certain Miss Egry's house, and I asked him to call for me and the big snub didn't. What would you do with a guy like that? I should have given him up right away.

To continue with my story:

I seem to remember a bazaar (Hungarian Festival) the church had in a place called Rockaczi Hall. This girl that I knew went with her mother and dad against her wishes and when she got there, the Pennsylvanian fellow was there working and wanted me to work there too.

I can't recall why, but I know that I was mad at something and refused to work there. Well, I walked around and met a fellow that I had seen around the other church affairs and spoke with him for a while. Then I saw another fellow who had come down to the choir once or twice and who belonged to the Young People Society. I passed him once or twice and then stopped to talk with him. We went over to one of the games and started to play the game. To my surprise, we were very lucky and kept winning one game after another. Well, not being a good businesswoman, I kept playing until I broke even in the end. I think I only had fifty cents in the beginning.

The young man asked me to allow him to take me home from

the affair and I told my mother that I would get a ride home and she could go home if she wanted to, and I would be alright. So, we hung around a bit and then he drove me home. I was so glad that for once I had actually met a man who didn't expect me to kiss him just for bringing me home. I knew that I was going to like this fellow.

Another incident which is very clear in my mind is a date I had to go to a particular game called basket-ball at the YMCA and I was supposed to watch a fellow whom I was acquainted with, from Pennsylvania. A fellow named Lou Toth took me to this affair. It rained cats and dogs, but we went just the same. Many of the boys from the choir and from the church whom I was familiar with were on this team. I always enjoyed the game, and I was kind of thrilled to think that the new fellow that I had just met was to be my escort. We got wet going in his car, but the game was well. During intermission, the Pennsylvanian came up and suggested that we go out to the park and have something to eat after the game, and it sounded like a swell time.

The end of the game came, and we went down into the main hall and waited for a little while and to my surprise, the new fellow who had escorted me didn't seem too anxious to wait for him, so we finally left by ourselves. Well, it rained so hard that we didn't bother getting out of the car. We just rode around the park and then suddenly the car had something wrong with it. I wonder what it could have been. I still haven't found out yet, just what was wrong. He said that the engine had died out. We had loads of fun because I knew, or at least I was hoping, that he was just kidding. It was still raining quite hard out and I didn't feel much like walking. He tried to get my ring off my finger, and I fought against it. Finally, he knocked it out of my hand, and it fell to the floor of the car and then I got mad. It was finally found between the seat and the door.

I got home at 2:20 that morning and mother couldn't imagine what had happened to me that night because she knew that I never stayed out very late and made it a rule to come home for 12:00 midnight.

Speaking of midnight, reminds me of another incident.

I went out with the two young men one night and told them I had to be home on the dot of 12:00 midnight. Well, we were still in the Little Hungary and it was very, very close to midnight, and I was quite nervous about going home. We finally left the place and had only a few minutes to get home in time. They drove me right into the backyard and it was exactly 12:00 midnight and I complimented them on getting me home on time. Then he backed out of the yard and I asked him where he was taking me and he said he had promised to get me home for midnight, but that didn't mean that I was going up into the house.

We drove around the block a couple of times and then they finally took me home. If I am not mistaken, the Pennsylvanian was the one to walk me to the back door, and he tried awful hard to kiss me goodnight, but was quite unsuccessful. Then he went out to join the other fellow, who I supposed had to take him home.

Finally, this Lou Toth defrosted a little and became more friendly. It took him quite a long time and, in the meantime, he had made a remark about blondes, which he said that he had been warned against blondes by a friend of his in the factory.

The three of us had made quite a number of trips together. We had a swell time, but I kind of hoped that we could have one date alone. We had gone to South Norwalk together and to dinner at the Little Hungary and up to Waterbury to see one of Bert's friends.

The fun began one night when Lou brought me home and we sat in his car in front of my house and had said goodnight so many times that it wasn't even funny. Then Lou dared to kiss me for the first time. After that I could hardly wait till the time passed between dates. They seemed like an eternity.

Lou had some funny ideas in his head about not being good enough for me to keep company with. I don't know where he got them from. It got me mad every time he would say it. Because I kept telling him if I didn't like him, I would never have started to go out with him.

There is something that I never knew about him and when this war is over, I have so many questions to ask him about himself. Somehow, I never was sure whether he would feel the same after he came home from battle, so I didn't count so much on it. I really can't explain it, I mean the way I felt, but I think you know because I remember in one of your letters of you telling me that you weren't sure yourself if this was the real thing.

There is an old saying about "Absence makes the heart grow fonder—for someone else." I don't think this is true at all. Since you went away, I went out with Julia Gyana and her cousin, and every time I was out with them, I couldn't talk of anything else except you, all the time. So, of all the fellows I know, there are none that compare with you, dear.

I had a swell time with Lou when we went to Coney Island together. I think that was one of the most embarrassing moments in my life. We were waiting to go on one of the rides and Lou told me I had a bloody nose, and I never even knew it. I had never had a bloody nose before and didn't even know I had one at the time.

I'll never forget the time Lou took me down to New York and he had intentions of taking me to meet his family and I didn't know it until I was already in New York and in the subway on the way to the Bronx where his father and sister and brother-in-law were waiting to see what I looked like. I don't need to tell you that I guess I was never in a tighter spot than I was at that moment.

Well, I managed to get to the house where his sister lived and I got up to the door and I met them, each in their own turn and was I relieved to see that they were very, very nice people and didn't treat me like a stranger at all. We had a swell time while we were there and then in the afternoon we went down to Central Park and took pictures and walked through the park and then we walked all the way down to the Loew's State Theatre on Broadway and we were pretty tired by then so we went in to see the show.

I remember it was a very sad picture and, being very emotional, I cried through most of the picture. That was one thing that I was always ashamed of, that was when I would cry in the movies.

By this time, I knew Lou fairly well and my family were determined that he was the very nicest fellow that I have ever gone out with. The reasons I liked him so much were because he was very neat and always came to my house dressed nicely and I knew he was a good fellow because he attended church regularly with me and didn't use profane language.

Some of the other characteristics I liked about him was that he didn't drink or smoke. You have no idea how much I admire a man who can keep himself from these bad habits. That is all they are, bad habits. None of them are necessary. I don't do them myself and I can't stand girls that do smoke or drink incessantly.

There are so many good things that I could enumerate, that probably would fill ten or twelve pages of writing, so I will save them all up and tell him when he comes home, and we have nothing to do some nights. Those are the nights that I am sitting home here waiting for now. All the girls are going out and having dates, even the ones that are married, but I don't like that, so I will wait patiently here until you come home to me. At least I won't have any regrets, and I know that I am waiting for something worthwhile. The ones here are married or they aren't worthwhile having, anyway.

We'll have so much to talk about when you come home. I can hardly wait till the day comes when I see you walking down my street and hear the bell ring and you're waiting to come in. We will have fun, won't we? I promise you we will never discuss the war unless you care to do so, on your own accord. I know if I saw the horrors you probably have experienced, I wouldn't want to talk about them, but some people say it is good to get some things off your chest, then you feel better. So if you want to talk about it, I will listen, but if you never mention it, I won't say a word about it.

I will have all I want, just having you come home safely to me and I will be content to spend a very quiet life wherever we may settle down until you have recovered sufficiently enough to find the thing that you will want to do for a living. I have kind of worried about that too. I have often worried, or I should say wondered, what you would turn to when you come home.

Martha absolutely loved writing and dreamed of being a writer, too. I thought of typing this out, but thought it would be much better to see the typewritten copies. One big takeaway from this was that Martha loved Louis—Grandpa Hiyi—unconditionally; so much so that she promised to never ask him about the war if he never brought it up. She knew it would be a difficult thing for him to talk about. Martha and Louis were my dream couple. I may have never met Martha because she died before I was born, but I hoped someday I would be in a relationship like she had been in. There were many silly stories about Martha. One, for instance, was that Martha was petrified of ever driving a car—keep in mind that cars were also kind of new at this point. Therefore, Grandpa drove her where she needed to go, or she would take the bus to work. One day, Martha and Louis' children were at the kitchen table and Martha yelled, "You have to go to school, and I have to go to work. Quick! Quick! I am running late!" Martha took a plate in her hand to put away and was rushing around like a madwoman and bonked the youngest child, Nancy, in the face. Nancy wasn't hurt but all the children looked up at her with a goofy look on their face. As soon as the kids were off to school, Martha put on her coat and went running out in her high heels to catch the bus! The long blue coat she wore trailed behind her as the wind blew it up like a parachute. "Wait for me, wait for me!" she yelled as she ran down the sidewalk toward the bus stop. The kids all laughed their way to school that morning. This was a typical morning for Martha.

Louis and Martha were not rich, but it did not take much to make them happy. Louis' sister, Helen, lived down in Florida still and the whole family would take the car to go down to visit her. There would be three in the front of the car and three in the back. Louis would always be the driver and in the middle, one unlucky kid was stuck between the focused driver and the extremely nervous front passenger, Martha. The other two children sat in the back and Louis' father, John, sat there too.

This small car might as well have been packed with clowns, as there was no air conditioning on the way down and then back up from Florida. In the backseat, Great Grandpa John would fall asleep right away as if the heat put him out and he had been in a sauna. His body would fall this way and that, with every single turn the car made. The kids always braced themselves if the turn was toward them as Great Grandpa John would fall over on them at that point and they would be working together to push him back upright again. In the front, Louis would be focused and mostly ignore all the gibberish going on in the car, but Martha would put out her arm every time he had to stop as if a kid was going to go flying. Louis' saying was, "Green means go, red means stop, YELLOW MEANS GO LIKE HELL!" So you can see why Martha may have been a nervous wreck. In any case, when they ended up making it down to Florida, it was a hell of a time.

There have been many stories shared about Grandpa Hiyi and Martha, but I still have many of my own to share as well.

I was at the kitchen table of his raised ranch doing a Snow White puzzle when he came up from behind and took one ponytail in each hand and said, "Giddyup!"

"Grandpa!! What are you doing?!" I shrieked and put one hand on each ponytail, stopping the puzzle right away. He laughed as he seemed to get a kick out of it and then sat a few seats away from me to play solitaire. He would shuffle the deck once...twice...maybe a third time, then put his cards out for Solitaire. After he'd play that, he sometimes repeated it, then would get up and walk around. At this point, I grew interested in his game.

"How do you play?" I asked. And he invited me to watch and learn. He took back all his cards so he could shuffle and show me from the beginning. He split the cards into two piles and shuffled them together a few times and then started by placing one card up then six faced down. Then, he would put a card facing up on the next card that had been faced down and then put five more faced down on top of the rest. He would repeat this until he reached the seventh column. From the deck, he flipped three cards at a time, and he could use this to put in an order of Ace - King. The goal was to have all the cards of the same suit starting at Ace in separate piles from the main game. If you found an Ace, you would put it over to the side and then once you found a two of the same suit, you would place that on top of that Ace card. It would continue on until all four Ace decks got up to King. Eventually, I followed in his footsteps and copied exactly what he would do when playing cards.; shuffling the deck and setting them out for solitaire again and again. "Hey, are you hungry, Grandpa?" I had asked.

He nodded his head but continued playing cards as if it didn't bother him either way. I had been really young and often experimented with food, thinking it was a great idea when maybe it wasn't so much. So, there I went in the kitchen and found whatever I could that looked like it would go well together. I pulled out a bag of bagels and then I found a can of little baby shrimps in the cupboard along with some butter. I pulled out the toaster and lightly toasted the bagels, then put them on plates. From here, I grabbed a butter knife and spread the little baby shrimps on each side of the bagels and BON APPÉTIT, that was my house special. As soon as I made it, I called everyone—to include my mom, Grandpa Hiyi, and his daughter, Grandma Neenee—to the kitchen table. They came out, and I placed the three-plated feast on the table.

They all came around and sat down but wouldn't say a word. They seemed to be smirking or holding in something that was uncontrollable. After sitting there for a few minutes, my mom finally asked, "Why don't you have a plate?" and I had said, "I am the chef. I am cooking for you." She seemed to gulp and then looked back down at her food. Grandpa, on the other side, had finished half a bagel and didn't seem to care much about the contents of what was on it. That was my beginning as a chef!

When I was younger, my parents had separated quite a few times. This is one reason why I had spent a great deal of time with my extended family on both sides. I will always remember the three sentences that Grandpa would say even through his dementia. He did not mean to offend.

"When are we going to feed the Indians?"—When will we go to the casino and give them all our money?

"Where is the moonshine?"—He was not a drunk in any way, but this was still quite silly.

"Are we going to the boondocks?"—Are we going far away? After a while, I caught on and would ask these questions right back at him. He smiled each time.

I put the pencil down that felt as though it was sliding out of my hands from writing so much and took a deep breath.

"See you next week?" Cece asked. I nodded.

# 4

# PINWHEELS

As I grew older, I realized how little materialistic things truly mattered. These things can be replaced, but they still reminded me from time to time of different things that had happened in the past. Both sides of my family were really into cooking and their cooking styles were extremely different, which made them each unique. When I got out of high school, I intended on going into culinary and was very excited about this. The goal was to have a catering company of some sort. After working in the school's restaurant my senior year, I still loved cooking and baking, but wanted to keep it as a hobby so my love for it would continue.

In my apartment, I would play through various records I had from my Grandma Neenee, but I would mostly look for Italian music. This night, I would play "Volare" by Dean Martin and some other great ones that I had made a playlist for. The recipe was going to be salmon with parmesan heavy cream sauce over white rice. I loved this simple recipe so much! First, I grabbed the salmon from the fridge and cut each filet in half so they could soak up the sauce much easier. After that, I cooked the salmon on both sides and put them on a plate for later. In the same pan, I put some minced garlic and onion, being careful not to burn it. I would put some baby spinach in right away. It is surprising how you could put in several handfuls of baby spinach only for it to shrink while cooking and seem like you hadn't put much in to begin with.

I waited for this to cook in the pan a bit and wilt when I noticed my cat, Milo, reaching up on his hind legs as if he wanted to help me cook—probably just taste it, though!

"Milo, no no no," I had said while dancing next to him a bit. He did not like this very much, but ended up jumping onto the chair a few feet away. Milo is a tabby cat with a white belly and white paws. He had black and gray stripes on the rest of his coat. I had rescued him along with Cleo, a black and white kitty. It was one of the best decisions I ever made in my life. This rescue meant lifelong friends that I would never forget.

When the spinach was wilted, I put in a bunch of chopped cherry tomatoes (IT MUST BE CHERRY OR GRAPE TOMATOES, sweeter the better) and poured in the heavy cream along with some parmesan. I always found an excuse to sprinkle some paprika in, so I went ahead and did that. One time, I tried to season this sauce with red pepper flakes and my mouth felt like it was flaming. Never again. After all this, I just put the salmon back in and put the temperature to a simmer with the top on the pan to let all the flavors soak right in. This is great over white rice.

I didn't have therapy that night, but couldn't help but think of my Nonna and felt the urge to write about her. The smell from the cherry tomatoes brought back so many memories of her house as she was always cooking up some kind of homemade sauce. I took out some paper:

Some days, I just remember waking up on my Nonna's couch. I hadn't even realized my mom carried me to the car wrapped in a blanket, and back out of the car once we reached her place and brought me inside. My parents both worked each weekday, so

Nonna would watch me. The comfort of several crocheted blankets she had made felt like it was just the same as home had been. I remember when I would wake up, I would go upstairs to her kitchen. She had a raised ranch with kitchens on both floors and seemed to have a routine where she would have breakfast upstairs and dinner in the downstairs kitchen unless it was winter. During that time, it was often too cold to eat downstairs and, since heat rises, we would find ourselves in the upstairs kitchen. I didn't mind either way.

I distinctly remember her pouring a bowl of cheerios for me as I looked through the comic portion of the Sunday newspaper from the weekend before. I would talk to her about the funny cartoons I found until the cheerios stood before me with a sprinkle of sugar...maybe more than just a sprinkle on top. That was the only way I knew to eat cheerios other than buying honey nut, but I had thought that was what everyone did from a very young age. Nonna's house was big for just her as my Nonno died when I was only about four years old. I do not remember him much, but I did have one memory of him, though. He seemed to be playing cards and was sitting down, otherwise he completely towered over me. I ran over and he pretended to steal my nose between his fingers and pulled away. Both of my hands went right to my face, touching and feeling for my nose that had just been taken! I was just a kid, of course I believed this!! When I discovered he was joking, we both laughed. That is the one memory I have of Nonno, but I remember it fondly. Most of my life, I had known Nonna to be in that house alone, but would often hear stories of Nonno. He was a hard-working man and would have done anything for his family, which was how he raised my father to be like. Nonno and Nonna went back and forth from Italy to America, as they were trying to decide whether or not it would be a good decision to move to America permanently. Nonna told me she waited for him for a very long time and then finally he had come back and they decided to go. Back in that day, they had to take ships to and from. Nonna was pregnant on the way to America, and I could only imagine how that was on top of sea sickness.

When I was at Nonna's house, I wouldn't wander much, but if I slept overnight, I found it to be very peaceful in her spare room. She always had a made bed in the quiet room and didn't have more furniture or clunky things than she needed. She lived within her means, not above. She had a very large poster of all the saints from over the years, as she was very religious. I never quite understood how someone could be so religious at the time. Whenever I had gone to church with her, I grew bored. But after a while, I saw many things were out of our control in life and being with God helped to make the unknown that much more bearable. It served as a constant and I guess everyone had their own reasons. She would also crack jokes at times and do silly things. One time, we were going to be late for dinner with the family (I was older) and I told her about this. She just said, "No, no…just tell them because I am old that I forgot." We both knew she didn't forget and she was using her age to her ADVANTAGE! Have you heard of someone doing that?! From when I was a child, all the way through high school, Nonna has had chickens. In fact, I am embarrassed to admit, we used to refer to her as "Chicken Nonni" since I had two nonnis.

Nonna is one of my biggest role models in my life. She had a difficult life, but also many joys that came through from her persistence and will to have a good life. Growing up, Nonna lived through World War II. Her father had just come back from serving and her entire family was overjoyed, but one day there was a missile that was sent down in their backyard in Italy and the shrapnel hit her father, killing him on impact. She was there to witness it, along with her siblings and mother. She could have just given up right there and then, but Nonna was much better than that and knew her father would have wanted her to muster on. So there she was in the kitchen, making Easter Bread in April and other foods that many of the ingredients came from her garden right in her backyard.

One of the most memorable foods that brings back many memories of my Nonna is a box of Pinwheels. Pinwheels look just like they sound. They are a type of pasta that you can buy from the store and use for soups or even in sauces. Nonna was the first one to introduce me to these, and I loved them ever since. I would sit there in her kitchen and eat them. We didn't even have to be talking, and it still felt like there was so much warmth and company there, even in our silence. One thing that I need to remind myself of is her words that she was proud to share: "Marissa always got her work done and never had to be told to do things for school. She always did them and then wanted to help." I think these are words I will always remember because it reminds me I may be that much closer to being as amazing as she was.

I smiled to myself as this seemed to make all the memories come to life again. There was a tear that traced down my cheek, but Milo had hopped right up onto my lap and curled up to make himself comfortable. Sometimes, it was the simplest of things that made it all seem ok.

# 5

# WINTER WONDERLAND

I laid in bed and felt something buzz from under my pillow. It couldn't be my alarm because that made a sound like a harp that got louder and louder the longer you let the alarm go on. Ask me how I know. I reached under and felt the very edge of the phone, but couldn't get it in time before it fell to the ground, making a loud thud. Milo, who laid in the nook of my legs, jumped up and looked around to see what the noise had been. I let out a big sigh and reached to the ground to retrieve the phone. To my surprise, there was a message from the county public schools:

"This is your county public schools announcing that there will be no school today due to the snow. Please stay tuned for updates about tomorrow and be safe today!"

This was one of the very, very, very nice things about being a teacher. I wanted to snuggle up to Milo back in bed, but had to use the bathroom. On my way back, I went over to the couch in the living room area and saw the winter wonderland my window displayed. It was as if I was looking into a whole other world, like in Narnia. I could open the window and just be in another place. The simplicity and gentleness of the snow falling onto the already coated ground provided me with a calm that I needed much of lately. Coming from Connecticut, there were many memories that I had in the snow. I grabbed my notebook and began writing.

The snow days at home were always some of the best. Often, I would be at home with my dad, but my mom would be there too sometimes if she didn't have to go to work. I wouldn't sleep in very often as I would rush downstairs and get breakfast so I could play outside as soon as possible. My dad would start plowing with his truck, but I'd be sure to have hot cocoa ready for him when he came back. Sometimes, I would even go with him. This was one of those times.

Dad was always on the go and walked past me as he said, "Slim, you wanna come with me to plow some driveways?" The answer would always be yes. I never hesitated to spend more time with him, and my mom would probably be back from work by the time we were back, anyway. I already happened to be in my snow boots and just needed to put on my jacket. Dad had my jacket in his hands; he must have gotten it from upstairs, as if he already knew that I would have said yes, no matter what. He helped me get into it by putting one arm in and then the other. Although he was a big guy, he was still very gentle with me, as if I was a toothpick that could easily break. When we walked out to his truck, he always walked to my side and scooped me up to put me in the front passenger seat.

"Alright, you wanna be the controller?" he asked. I trusted him so, of course, said yes even though I had no clue what that entailed. He handed me a small device that had a few buttons. It had a main part that was shaped like a rectangle with four buttons on it, then had a long bar on the top with a few more buttons.

"What does this one do?" I pointed to one of them. He was an impatient guy, but for me he somehow had all the patience in the world.

"See the arrows? The arrows make the plow go up, down, left, and right. The ones on top drop the plow down when we need to collect snow and then bring it back up when we have snow in the plow so we can put it in a pile away from the driveways. You got this, Slim." I wasn't so sure about that, but thought I could give it a try. Why not! Dad was settled in the driver's seat of his truck and turned the key in the ignition. The start could probably be heard down the street as it was a diesel truck and had a loud exhaust that blared through the neighborhood, telling exactly who was passing by! I liked it because it alerted me whenever he was home. As we drove, he talked the whole way. My dad was a talker and would enjoy telling stories about different things that happened. I guess I could see where I got it from.

"Do you remember the time we were at Santa's land with Mom and you were on the sled? Oh, Slim, it was so bad what happened! I was at the bottom of the hill taking pictures and recording when your genius mother put you at the top on the sled to go down by yourself. You usually went down with her, but nope, not this time. I told her she should be sitting on the long sled with you, but she just said, 'Joey, she'll be fine!' and don't ask me why I listened to that. So, I'm recording, right, and you were coming down from the top while we were at the bottom cheering you on. You picked up so much speed in the sled probably because you weighed close to nothing and Mom put out her foot and wham, the sled stopped abruptly and you went flying out of it headfirst into a snowbank."

"We've gotta get her for doing that! What!" I screamed.

He laughed so hard at what I said.

"Let's get her with snowballs when we go home! Come on!" I continued, amped up by the story he told me. He continued laughing while he turned down a street and lost some speed.

"Alright, press the top button to drop it," he said, and I listened. I heard the plow drop to the ground. He moved forward with his truck slowly, as I assumed it collected snow along the way. "Okay, click the button next to it to pick the plow up," he said. These were simple directions that I could easily get. He never said anything that was too complex for me and always made sure I could understand. I followed again. "See, there you go! You got this!"

We continued the same routine for the entire driveway and by the time we got to the next one, I didn't need any directions from him whatsoever. We were a good team, and that's why I always enjoyed coming along with him, but this was the first time that I went on this kind of adventure where I was the controller of the plow. Sometimes, he would sit me on his lap and go slowly while pushing my fingers into the buttons. This was when I was really young and couldn't see over the dashboard as well. I still barely could.

On the last driveway, he told me how we were going to get home and then hide out in back to throw snowballs at my mom. I couldn't wait. I looked over at the clock on his truck and it had said 3:45. She may be home at this point, who knows. Dad turned some music on and his CD went to one of his favorite songs that he would sing in the car to me while I just sat there, embarrassed. The song was "Lovin'" by Journey. He blasted the song and took my small arm in his, waving it left and right as if

I was conducting the music. I always turned bright red when he did this. Now I know this is a song for a couple, but he would use it as an excuse to tickle me or squeeze my arm and thought it was the funniest thing ever.

We finally pulled into our driveway, and I saw Mom's dark brown Pontiac Grand Prix, which has since been discontinued. It was always such a girly looking car, no offense to any guys who had it, but I always thought that the body of it was very delicate looking and fashionable. I don't know. Anyway, as soon as he parked, he shushed me and snuck around the back of the car to the front passenger side, where I was.

"Shh, let's sneak out back and hide behind that snowbank, Slim," he said. I hunched my shoulders and took big steps behind him, but still tip toed the whole way. The snow had been heavy, but there was no ice, so I didn't have to worry about slipping. I started to giggle when we made it behind the snowbank. I put one hand over my mouth to contain my laughter. The back door opened...

"Hello? I know you guys are there, your truck just pulled up!" Mom said. Dad continued to shush me, but I couldn't help giggling and I could tell he was trying to hold in his laughter too. He was also busy making snowballs. Mom came out a little farther and had her coat on, continuing to say, "Hello?"

"Alright, on three," Dad whispered as he handed me a snowball.

"One...two...THREE!" He went running out and pelted Mom right in the stomach. She bent over.

"Ow! That's not right, what was that for?!" she said. He continued to gather more snowballs and pelted her again and again. I did the same, but didn't seem to throw it as fast as he did. I thought it would be silly to pelt one at Dad even though we were always on the same team. This time, I actually hit him right on the shoulder.

"Oh, you're going down!" He turned to me and ran over, scooping me up and placing me on top of the snowbank so that my feet were stuck in there. He pelted me over and over again, but not too hard. I couldn't stop laughing and was trying so hard to run, but my legs were stuck, and it made Dad laugh even more.

"Come on, get her out of there, that's not fair!" Mom said. After a few more, he had his fun and picked me up out of the snowbank.

"Thought we were supposed to be on the same team, Slim!" he said. I just kept laughing uncontrollably.

Snowy days were some of the best days in my family. At times, when people had no choice but to stay in together, they found themselves getting on each other's nerves. We really didn't have this when I was young. I continued to look outside and decided to make some hot cocoa and put on Harry Potter as I would normally do.

# 6

# OLDIES & DOO-WOP

It had been several days since the snow came down, leaving the town covered in a soft white blanket. When it came down over here, it sometimes took days for the snow to melt and cleanup to be done. I went to meet Cece at her office again and was thinking about things to write about the whole way. My thoughts kept straying away from certain memories as I still had a brick wall keeping them out. I knew I would have to face those memories someday but wanted to continue sticking to the good ones for now. I just wasn't ready yet.

I pushed on the brake slowly as my car crept toward the stop sign right before the turn for the office. The clock read 10:45 a.m. and I still had fifteen minutes until the appointment began. There was no middle ground for me when it came time to be somewhere. I was either really early or late. I could never seem to be exactly on time. When you have somewhere to be, you never know if there will be traffic, construction work, or just something else that comes up. In my case, if I did not leave super early—there was surely at least one obstacle that came up, causing me to be late. The brick building was set aside from the rest of the plazas and had a big parking lot. Many therapists and other professionals rented out rooms within; I assumed that's why there was a huge parking lot. Instead of going in and waiting in the lobby, I pressed the lever on the side of my seat to recline a little and closed my eyes as I listened to the radio. My ears were suddenly filled with Kenny Vance's soft voice. "Life Could Be a Dream… if I could take you up to paradise up above, if you could tell me that I'm the only one you love…"

I felt a tear trickle down my cheek as my eyes remained closed and my mind took me back to my Nonni and Nonno's—the Italian side of my family.

Growing up, I only lived about ten minutes away, give or take, from their house. They lived in the next town over and it was really nice to be so close to them because I found myself there quite often. I never wondered what my parents would do for the day while I was away at their house, but always looked forward to a similar routine each time. Dad would drop me off and I'd have all my sleeping stuff that I would put upstairs in the bedroom. Even when I could drive myself when I got older, I still slept over there time and time again. This time, we were going to wake up early the next day to go somewhere special, then stay the night. I was so excited! As soon as I walked into their house, I saw the brownie box on the counter and knew that Nonni had it out for me so we could make some brownies. It just always felt comfortable being there. Nonno was in his chair in the living room, watching the news. Occasionally, he would have Maury or Divorce Court on, but not when Nonni was home, because she didn't really go for those shows. Another guilty pleasure of his was the Real Housewives shows. I liked when he had them on; not because of the actual show itself, but because it was always entertaining to watch him talk at the TV and do his hearty laugh each time he thought something was funny. I could spend hours sitting on the couch near him as he watched these shows.

I gave Nonni a kiss on the cheek to say hello and quickly went over to Nonno and kissed him on the cheek. "Hey Nonno, are you excited to go tomorrow?" I asked. We would be going to Mohegan Sun—the nearby casino—to attend a Doo Wop show. What in the heck is Doo Wop? Well, you haven't fully lived if you don't know it... Doo Wop music is basically oldies, but it is called 'Doo Wop' because of the background singers as they always joined in chorus as they sang different words like "Doo Doo Dooo wop wop wop." Ok, I sound crazy explaining it like this, but the music is very uplifting and that is why I liked it. No one I know likes the music and laughs at me when I talk about it, but it also brought me closer to my grandparents because I knew they enjoyed that music a lot. When they listened to it, it really brought them back to their childhood/teenage years, which were so different. They didn't have phones for each person back then, which seemed to cause more people to talk to one another, as there would be an awkward silence in the room if they didn't talk. They also had this amazing small amusement park right on the water! The park was at the West Haven beach and there were even some rides that went over the water. (Not sure how that was safe, but whatever!) If you go to the Savin Park Museum, you can see pictures from back in the day when they still had the park. Imagine that. Living near a park that is right on the beach and being able to soak up the sun and jump in the water right afterward. Whenever I closed my eyes to picture this, the Doo Wop music ALWAYS played and there was cotton candy... it just seemed like such a great time that they lived in.

"Girllll, are you ready for the concert?! I know I am!" he

said with a smile on his face after he brought his attention back to the TV. I walked back over to the kitchen area and was ready to make the brownies and just lay on the couch in the room with Nonno.

"Did you wash up already?" Nonni asked. She liked to have me wash up at night, so the next morning I didn't have to worry about getting sick if I left with a wet head. That would actually not be allowed at her house. Even if I wasn't zipped up all the way, they would make sure to correct it. That's just who they were—they cared so much. I shook my head, a little bit annoyed because I wanted to just get right into making the brownies.

"Alright, go on up and I can do your hair when you get out. I already set the bed for you," she called after me as I already made my way up the stairs. I was quick to set my bags down in the room, grab my pajamas and things out so I could just switch into them after the shower. I definitely had a sweet tooth and Nonni knew it—knowing I would be down soon after to have the brownies. I bet she already got started on them, too. As soon as I showered and slipped on my pajamas, I squeezed my hair out in the towel and brought it downstairs with a comb and two hair ties. Nonni liked to do French braids in my hair when I got out of the shower. It was easy because it would be out of my face and the next day, I'd already have my hair done. When I walked into the living room area where Nonno was still sitting, I noticed Nonni moved a chair in the center of the room for me to sit in.

"Here, sit right here—I'll fix your hair." I followed right away and started talking to Nonno.

"So tell me, girl, how's everything going?" he asked. He was always so interested in my life and asked about me and how my dad was doing, too.

"It's going good. How are you Nonno? Are we going to get Pepe's pizza tomorrow when we go to Mohegan Sun? This is going to be so much fun!" I exclaimed as I winced a bit from the comb pulling out a knot in my hair as Nonni braided it. "Do you want to watch something?" I asked.

"Oh, your grandmother already has something all picked out to watch tonight. Girl, wait till you see this. You'll love this movie!" he said as he grabbed the remote.

Nonni continued doing my hair but started talking about the movie, "It's called The Perfect Gift. You heard of that?" I shook my head. "Well, you'll see. It's a really good movie. I don't want to give it away too much, but it's with the older man that was in The Notebook movie." Nonni always picked out wholesome movies, kind of similar to Hallmark movies. But I liked the stories that they gave and seemed to always have a lesson to go along with them as well.

"Alright Fred, put it on," she said as he was trying to look closely at the remote to figure out which button he had to press again to switch over to the movie. Nonni had just finished braiding my hair, and I always liked to feel the back of each braid because it was really cool. When my hair dried like this, if I took it out the next day, I would have wavy hair.

The TV shut off. "Freddie, give me the remote," she said. I giggled and Nonno looked over at me with a look that said a thousand words. He looked like he would've been sayin', "Nonni knows everything. I'm just an old fart here." He had such a silly way of talking and the two of them together were even better because it was like night and day with them, but they made it work. Within a few minutes, Nonni had the TV back on and the movie was already starting.

"Hey, shouldn't we do the brownies?" I asked.

"No, no. I got it. I want you to watch this; it's very good," Nonni said as she went off into the kitchen.

I lay back on the couch while Nonno was in his recliner chair, and the movie began. Nonno always nodded off a few minutes after the movies would begin, but this time I was actually quite interested from the moment it began.

The movie was basically about this family that was born into wealth and the great grandfather who was the one to come into all the riches to share with his family was dying and left a will. At the table with lawyers, his whole family fought over everything, and they were so surprised that the will did not include them in much. The grandson found out he wasn't even left a dollar and stormed out of there. Later, the grandfather's lawyer had said that there were certain conditions that the grandfather left in the will and that the grandson had to do these things that were outlined in the will to receive anything.

At first, the grandson was quick to not do anything, but then realized he really wanted the potential money that he could get. The series of conditions were things that could cause the grandson to appreciate life more and money less. They were things such as helping on a farm for hours and hours in the hot sun, going to another country that barely had anything and helping over there, et cetera. One of my favorite parts was when the grandson had his credit cards turned off and had nothing to his name and had to find a genuine friend, then bring them to the lawyer's office to prove this. Unfortunately, he went to all his "friends" that he had, but since he had no money to buy anything for them, they refused. He ended up lying down, homeless, in the park. A little girl came up to him and asked to be friends and the girl's mother accompanied her as well. At first, he was like no way. But then, as he talked to the mother and the girl more, he realized she needed a friend just as much he did. The girl had cancer and she planned to eventually set him up with her mom so she wouldn't be alone when the girl left. Long story short, he ended up working through all the conditions that were left for him and truly appreciate life more. He cut off his old "friends" as they weren't really friends to begin with and he worked more time in his life for the people who were true to him. At the very end, the grandfather had left his entire fortune to him as he passed all the tests.

This was a good movie because I feel it was relatable, as most people do truly seem money-oriented. Yes, money helps to provide stability and a place to stay. It surely does. However, some people let money get to their head too much and still end up unhappy in the grand scheme of things. Throughout the movie, I lost track, but must have eaten four or five brownies. They really hit the spot, and I was thankful for nights like these with my grandparents. It was simple and didn't need much, but I was thankful.

The next day, I woke up and made some pancakes. I heard the news come on from downstairs early in the morning. Nonni and Nonno were both early risers. We were getting everything ready, and I brought my bag down so we could stay overnight at Mohegan Sun. The concert was around three in the afternoon, so we would need to leave right after breakfast. (They were like me. There was no "in between" with them when it came to being on time. So, they were just VERY EARLY everywhere they went because you never knew what problems would come up.) After breakfast, we loaded everything into the car. Nonno got in the driver's seat as Nonni was in the front passenger and I was in the back. Nonni got a Doo Wop CD that she popped into the CD player in the car, and we prepped for this concert, listening to all the oldies. Mohegan Sun was about an hour and a half away, depending on traffic. So, you could imagine just how many songs we went through. Nonno requested we listen to his CD and in went Cher. Whenever I hear a Cher song, I think of him reaching out to the stage because I remember Nonni brought him to a Cher concert once and had said he kept trying to reach out to Cher on the stage. This was so funny to me.

The ride there went by kind of fast. It was always so beautiful when looking out the windows because the trees at this time of the year—almost spring—were just growing their leaves back again. You could tell you were close to Mohegan Sun by seeing all the different signs on the way. It would be hard to miss the turn. We had to pull into the hotel area first to drop everything off and check in. Then, we went right to the concert. I was excited to be here, but also look around after the concert too. Mohegan Sun was a special place for me because I studied it a lot when I was very little and learned about Native Americans. Few kids get to live so close to preserved relics and artifacts of the Native Americans.

The Doo Wop concert was directed and produced by "Bowser." No, not Mario's arch nemesis... Bowser was actually part of the Doo Wop group: Sha Na Na. If you ever watched the movie Grease before, they played some music throughout it and showed up as some of the characters. I guess he was trying to get some younger kids into Doo Wop music as he introduced the opening singer who was a young kid; probably around sixteen or seventeen years old and he started singing Doo Wop music. He was actually pretty good! After this opening act, there would be the actual Doo Wop groups that were still around, performing.

Bowser introduced the next mystery band as good friends of his who were eager to perform for us. Well, not just us...there was a whole crowd of people! Just as we thought we would have to guess the band, he said, "Jay & The Americans, coming right out!" and everyone cheered like wild. Some gentle strumming of a guitar led us right into Jay's voice as he began to sing "Come A Little Closer."

"In a little café just the other side of the border...she was sitting there and giving me looks that make my mouth water...so I started walking her way......lalalalalaaa."

I felt myself get up from my seat and just start dancing back and forth along with the music. Nonni did the same and Nonno clapped his hands together and sang. He knew every single word to the lyrics and didn't miss a beat! The thing about this music was that it was just so uplifting, but it also made me so happy to see my Nonni and Nonno happy from it, too. This was one of the best days I ever had with them in my life. We stayed there through the encores at the end. Normally, people would leave early so they could miss all the people traffic, but Nonni and Nonno didn't want to miss a second of this and neither did I.

We got our Pepe's pizza and shopped around for a bit. They didn't really play any slot machines or gamble as it was too much of a risk to be worth it. We went back to the hotel room, and I was ready for bed.

I noticed Nonno was in the main area of our hotel room, but Nonni wasn't there with him. I was just about to go to my bedroom when I sat next to him and said, "What's the matter, Nonno?"

He cried a bit as quiet as he could because he must've wanted to conceal it from Nonni.

"I just worry about your father so much. He doesn't answer me much anymore and I don't know what to do with him," he said as he put his head down. During this time in my life, my dad's health wasn't doing so well and the medications he had been on were now tolerant for him as he had to take more and more to take care of the pain he had in his leg from a military accident he was involved in. He would often sleep a lot of the time and seemed depressed. He stopped taking care of himself as much, and both my parents had split up, then gotten back together again quite frequently.

"I know Nonno, me too." I said, not knowing what else to say to him.

"You know, when he was born I said, 'This is my son. He's going to make something of himself that I couldn't. He could even be the President someday.' But look at it now," Nonno said.

"Nonno, you help a lot. You can only do so much. My dad is a good person. It doesn't matter what you have or what role you serve as your job, my dad has made something of himself," I reminded him.

"You're right, Rissa," he said. "Give Nonno a kiss on the cheek, ok? We're going to be leaving to go home first thing in the morning." I reached over and kissed his cheek, then gave him a hug and went off to bed.

A knock came at my window, and I was startled to see who it was. I must have fallen asleep. I saw Cece peering in from outside and she looked confused, but also concerned. I rolled down my window.

"Hey there! When you didn't show up, I tried calling you. Is everything ok?" she asked.

"Oh yeah, I'm ok! I just must have had a long week." I checked the time at it was 11:40. Therapy would be ending in five minutes. "Oh man, I am so sorry. I will still pay the copay for today. Can we reschedule?" I asked, apologetically.

"Sure thing! It happens! Let's do tomorrow same time if you can?" That was a Sunday, so I was off and would be able to. I nodded and apologized again, but I was happy to relive that memory with my grandparents

MARISSA D'ANGELO

# 7

# SURPRISE

I find myself spending a lot of time reminiscing about different things in the past. I can close my eyes and play back certain memories perfectly, as if I am watching a movie. The snow in the Northeast brought some great memories and Christmas seemed incomplete without it. I had a cousin the same age as me and our grandma would bring us to a Harry Potter movie and go through a Christmas lights drive through each year. This is something I really looked forward to. Grandma was a little bit kooky. There were so many stories about her. One of them was that she loved Elvis Presley so much that she drew his name and him on a van she had, only for the sun to beat down on it and make it permanently set into the van. Another silly story was that my dad had refused to bring her grocery shopping because it was snowing so…she put on her snow boots and took her wheelbarrow to walk to the grocery store and filled up her wheelbarrow to bring the groceries back home. When it wasn't snowing like crazy, she had a car that wouldn't go in reverse, so she had to park in spots that she would be able to continue driving forward to get out. She liked to play Italian music on her record player or even just on her radio as she'd cook. She'd just dance around the kitchen as she was cooking and that was her little slice of heaven on earth. She didn't have much money, but the experiences she brought me were nice. I remember we would plan it all out.

Each year, Harry Potter would come out in the theaters right around Christmas time. Grandma had an older thunderbird that had belonged to her father and was left to her. Olivia and I would pile into the backseat of the car and make ourselves comfortable. I'm not sure what we would be talking about, but I'm pretty sure grandma led most conversations asking about the movie and what we thought would happen...this and that...

"You guys are in for a treat tonight. We can stop at McDonald's after the movie, too!" grandma called back to us.

Olivia and I looked at each other and smiled. "Well, what do you think is gonna happen in this one?" I asked.

My cousin replied, "Well, in the last one, Lord Voldemort came and then Harry defeated him by using that stone. So maybe in this one he'll go back to Hogwarts and I wonder if Voldemort will come back." Olivia was very factual and outstanding in school; I knew she was just the person to ask. I definitely agreed with her on this, of course.

"Who knows, maybe Harry Potter is Voldemort," grandma stirred the pot.

"Yeah, okay, grandma," I said, knowing she was joking anyway. The car suddenly came to a slow crawl as I noticed we were in a line of cars. I looked outside and there were no movie signs whatsoever, but at the head of the line there was a little kiosk. Strange... I exchanged glances with Olivia. She looked just as puzzled as me. And if she was puzzled, that was surely saying something, as she usually knew what was going on.

"Umm, where are we?" she asked grandma. I could see grandma smiling in the rearview mirror. She wasn't gonna budge.

"Hey, I thought we were seeing Harry Potter!" I said,

disappointed.

"You'll see. We're still going!" Grandma replied, still having a devious grin from ear to ear. Well, it looks like she had this planned for a while, but still not sure what. The slow crawl of the line gradually brought us to the little kiosk, where a person was dressed in Christmas clothes. She had pointy elf ears that looked as if they were made of some kind of felt or some other material, a green button-down shirt with gold buttons. Her collar had candy cane stripes along it as well as her cuffs, and she had matching stockings and a skirt on. What was this?!

Grandma rolled down her window and handed the lady a five-dollar bill, which she accepted.

"Welcome to the Festival of Lights!" the lady shouted and peered in to say hello to us. "Come on in. Just make sure to follow the cars in front of you. Enjoy!" she said. Grandma drove on and as I turned back, I saw the lady continuing to wave to us before the next car came up in line.

"Alright kiddos, this is going to be really great. You'll love this!" grandma said. As she moved forward, we grew closer and closer to a bright entrance filled with assorted colors. It said, "Festival of Lights." It looked like a tunnel because all behind it up high were even more lights hanging across in lines. We were underneath all of them; it was like we were entering a whole other dimension. After the light tunnel, there were displays on each side. One of them over on Olivia's side was of penguins sledding. On the other side, snowmen were throwing snowballs. Some of the lights flickered and danced around while others remained bright. One of my favorite displays was the penguins that went fishing. Olivia and I were completely stunned by this as the backseat was quiet, not one peep was heard from us as our attention was sucked in by the show.

After several more displays, we seemed to have come to the end of the festival. Out of that sparkling dimension and back to the world.

"So, what'd you guys think?!" grandma asked.

Like clockwork, we both answered, "Can we go again?!" and we did. Grandma drove us through one more time and we went to the movie soon thereafter. We had finally had enough after the second go-around and went to see Harry Potter. We knew we'd be having McDonald's after, but had to load up on some popcorn and snacks. Olivia chose some sour candy while I chose the Buncha Crunch. That was my go-to! It was just so good. We filed into the theater with our goodies and found a seat toward the middle, but just close enough to the screen, and the movie started. It was funny because we always whispered to one another during the movie; I'm not even sure how we even knew what was going on half the time. This is how we knew we were happier just being together.

# 8

# STAGNANT

There had been a long lapse in time from when I last wrote in my journal. I think I had tired myself out completely from the last few chapters. It was difficult to think about the memories that were long gone. Every ounce of my being wished to relive them over and over again. Each time I went to see Cece, we talked instead of silence and writing. We mostly talked about what I had previously written and what was going on in the present for me. I liked our sessions because I didn't feel pressed too much. I could just continue talking about the good ol' happy days till I was ready. We did talk about some goals to set. This week, I needed to work on pushing myself to make time for myself and try to leave work at work. For anyone that knew me, this would be very challenging as I worked until I slept. There was one thing causing me to hold myself more accountable for this though—I signed up for a MeetUp in a group I belonged to for kayakers.

Normally, I just went on my own. It still felt so freeing. I knew I had to step out of my comfort zone, though. I drove about forty minutes or so to the Tidal Basin. This is a huge lake that is right next to the Washington Monument, Lincoln Memorial and a lot of other historical landmarks in Washington, DC. We were going for sunset, and I thought it would definitely be worth it.

I decided to go right from work since it was close to rush hour anyway, so I needed to give myself a lot of time. As I drove closer into

Washington, DC, I noticed a handful of tents here and there. I wondered if they were part of some kind of protest or something. I didn't really see anyone near the tents, though.

Eventually, I pulled up to a boathouse where they rented kayaks out to people along with canoes. I stayed in my car, unsure of the area. I felt jittery, which was unusual for me, but it had been so long since I actually went out with friends. To my left, a girl that looked familiar was alone, but she had two braids that went down just below her shoulders. Her dark features and tanned skin did look familiar. I checked the MeetUp app, and it was Tiana. As soon as I got out of my car, she came over and introduced herself. Another girl came over, Michelle, and we all began talking about our choice to come hang out that night.

I told them, "Well, I figured I would likely just watch Netflix or do work on the computer, so it was worth pushing myself to come out."

"Oh girl, I know what you mean. I spent the last winter without it, but I listened to music instead. Not sure how I managed without it!" she smiled.

"I have debated doing that, but sometimes I need the distraction from my own mind," I said. Michelle just kind of nodded and agreed with us.

"Alright guys, we gonna go?" she asked. They helped me get my kayak from my car and actually both rented a canoe together. As soon as I got in the kayak, they went in their canoe. Michelle and Tiana somewhat struggled to get in sync with one another as they each had a half of a paddle so one would have to paddle on either side. I thought it would make a perfect picture, so I quickly steered myself toward them and snapped a shot. Michelle was in front with her paddle up in the air as if she had just founded a new island and Tiana was in the back, smiling, but paddling normally. It was much slower than a kayak. I tried to stay back with them but ended up paddling toward the "Sister

Islands." They're just smaller pieces of land that poke out of the water, especially in low tide. It was high tide, so there wasn't much to them. The sun was just setting and a fiery mirror echoed in the water ahead of me. In this moment, was a calm. I thought about therapy the next time and I think I was ready to open that door I had shut for so long.

# 9
## ONE SMALL STEP

After kayaking, I hadn't really kept in touch with the girls. I'm not sure why, but it didn't bother me too much. Ever since that time on the water, I was counting down the days until my next session at therapy. I wasn't completely ready, but I at least wanted to make an attempt toward breaking down a wall that had been up for so long.

I had arrived ten minutes early that day to therapy, but instead of waiting in my car, I walked right into the waiting room, hoping she'd take me early. Worth a try.

She opened her door and commented on my time, "Hey, you're here early. Come on in. I had no appointments before you."

I walked in and she had my notebook waiting for me with a pen set aside. I sat down, but started by talking to her about my plan.

"This whole time, I have been writing about the happiest moments of my life. I am ready to dig into parts of my past that are not too happy. I want to let them go. I want to face them," I said.

Cece nodded in agreement and gave a warm smile. I wanted to tell one memory that began to shape me. One where I was on the brink of death...

The summer after I got out of kindergarten had been a hot one, but also very much a blur to me. I stayed in bed for most of the time. My mom would frequently stay home with me and press her hand up to my forehead to feel my temperature.

"You're burning up still," she said. I didn't flinch. She just brought me saltines and gave me Tylenol to try to keep my fever down. My parents did complement one another in this way. Whereas my dad was too sensitive and got upset when I was hurt or sick, my mom would patch up any cuts I had or pull my hair back if I was sick to my stomach. I admired this about their relationship.

After the fever had gone on for several days and nothing seemed to work, she brought me into the doctors. From there, I was rushed to the emergency room right away. I couldn't understand why. Both my mom and dad were by my side during this time. I was at Yale Children's Hospital. I remember only waking up in my hospital bed to be poked and prodded by the doctors. So much so that I had to choose an arm that I wanted most of my shots on as I ended up needing a cast at one point. I chose my left arm so I could still draw, hoping to have some sort of energy. The doctors had found that I had Kawasaki Disease. This is VERY RARE, and of course, I had to somehow get it. It starts with a rash and fever, but then if it is not caught in time, it will cause permanent heart damage.

During the day, my fever was mostly down, as I was on a lot of baby aspirin each day. At one point, I was allowed to go into the kid's playroom at the children's hospital. There were some very young kids playing with toy trains and other blocks, but what drew my attention instantly was the group of kids around the computer. These children did not have any hair, and I later found out that they all had cancer. I got along well with them though as I asked what they were playing, and they included me right away.

"We're playing Freddie Fish. You've gotta find the missing conch shells." I watched one of the kids play and he moved the fish about to locate the shells. Freddie fish was yellow with orange fins and big blue eyes. He looked so happy and this game definitely distracted me from what was going on. After a little bit, they let me have a turn on the game and I really fell in love with it. It was time to head back to our rooms, and I said goodbye.

Mom stayed with me each night while Dad watched the house, but he still was there a lot of the time. There was one night I remember where I couldn't stop shaking in my bed and it felt as though I was convulsing. The monitor I was hooked up to was beeping endlessly and doctors rushed in. I could tell my mom was a nervous wreck, as she must've just fallen asleep for the hour or so she could get. I was hooked up to more fluids and given more baby aspirins, but it was a Catch-22 because they couldn't give me too many baby aspirins, as it was damaging, too. After a week or so, I was starting to feel better, but due to the rash I had with the disease, my skin was completely peeling off all over my body. I felt so terrible and confused about what was going on. I felt like my skin had been burned off. Mom persisted on taking me to have a bath, but I kept refusing as I was already uncomfortable enough. She eventually did take me though, and the rash and skin issues subsided.

On one amazing day, my dad came in and brought Chinese food. They had previously been watching what I ate at the hospital, so this was strange that I was allowed Chinese food all of a sudden. He came in with it and a big smile from ear to ear. Both Mom and Dad were ecstatic, but I couldn't figure out why. Dad sat next to me. "I sold my car, Slim. We're going to Disney! You made it! We're leaving the hospital!" He gave me the biggest hug he could possibly give without breaking me in two, and I felt so happy and excited. My mom agreed to coordinate everything and plan the entire trip with an itinerary to make sure we made the most out of our vacation. The nurse came in shortly after and they handled the discharge paperwork. Before I knew it, I was on my way out with my parents. We made one quick stop before leaving the hospital, and that was the toy room. The nurse led us there and let me pick any toy I wanted: I chose Battleship. That was the first one my dad mentioned when we walked in, and I knew I wanted to play it with him.

I read this to Cece, and she was taken aback. This was a life-changing thing that happened to me so early in life, and I still somehow remembered a lot of it. When you go through a time where you're on the brink of death, it truly changes you. I had been young, but I still understood that there was something very bad happening and I was desperate for life to go back to normal again for me. I made it through, and I will remember this.

"That is a good memory, Marissa. Thank you for sharing that with me," she said. I nodded and smiled, feeling more weight coming off my chest.

"Did you guys end up going to Disney?" she asked, curious.

"Yes, we actually went on the Disney Cruise. I felt so bad though because my dad gave up his car in order to go with me. I know he really liked that car. But he told me no car or anything else mattered when it came to me." I said, feeling warm in my heart.

"That's so nice, Marissa. When you leave here today, I want you to continue focusing on doing what will make you happy, but this time I want you to write it down, ok?" she said. And so I did just that.

# 10
## ROAD TRIP

I am going to start this by saying my view of the most magical place on this planet was a place I would travel to almost every year by car and make a two-day trip down the East Coast to get to. The night before we would leave, my mom would have already packed her things, and she'd be helping me. We would all get to bed really early because, for some reason, the next day would begin around three in the morning. I was always completely full of excitement because I knew where we would be going. By some miracle, we managed to all get on the road by four at the latest. The car would've been packed up the night before and all they had to end up doing when I was really young was scoop me up and place me in the backseat to embark on our road trip. By the time I would wake up, I'd open and close my eyes a few times, then they'd burst open as soon as I remembered where we were headed. I was an only child and so my parents didn't really miss a thing. As soon as I shifted a bit in my seat, they'd notice.

"Hey Slim. You want some Mickey D's?" my dad would ask. Before I could answer, my mom would reply for me and say, "Yes! I bet she does, and I am starving!" My mom was like a twig, but also somehow a bottomless pit, too. Dad peered back in the rearview mirror to check with me. I nodded my head because I was pretty hungry. I even felt my stomach start to rumble.

So that was the consensus. We decided we'd get off the next exit and order a few egg sandwiches, as they were still serving breakfast at the time. Even for breakfast, my dad was notorious for ordering a coke.

After a while of driving on a straightaway, we got off an exit that had a sign on the entrance that displayed the McDonald's logo. We rolled up to the drive thru as Dad wanted to continue driving down and not waste much more time.

A lady's voice came out from the speaker box next to the giant menu. "How can I help you?" she asked, in a rushed manner.

"Yeah, I'd like one ham, egg, and cheese, then two bacon, egg, and cheeses. Make them a meal, please, with the hash browns." There was a pause, as I assume the worker was inputting the order.

"Drinks?" she asked. Dad paused and looked over at Mom. He already knew what he and I wanted, but Mom was fickle.

"Umm, do they have iced coffee?" she asked. It couldn't have been that simple, though. Dad turned to the speaker and ordered,

"I'll have a coke, OJ, and iced coffee."

Mom blurted out, "No, no. I'll have hot coffee." Dad took a deep sigh.

"You get that?" he asked. The lady confirmed and before we knew it, we were on our way again.

Dad made this trip often enough that not much seemed to faze him. Why didn't we just go down to Florida on a plane?

Well, my dad was in the army and was $82^{nd}$ airborne. After that, he was afraid to go on planes. People usually just want to rush from point A to point B, but these road trips were an even better time to be together.

By the time everyone finished their meals, Mom had the giant, foldable paper map spread across the front right side of the car, and we had continued on. When Dad knew where he was going, she'd tuck the map away but usually do her makeup. There was one point where she had some kind of cream foundation that she was putting on and they hadn't checked on me in the back in a bit. The next time they had looked back, my entire face was covered in white from the cream cheese bagel I had been eating at the time. Dad was looking back at me from the middle rearview mirror, and I could see he didn't even know what to say, but his face turned bright red as if he was going to burst out with laughter at any moment.

"I put on makeup like Mommy." And I suppose that was enough to make her stop caking on foundation. It's little moments like this that just can't happen on a plane as much as on a road trip.

# MARISSA D'ANGELO

# 11
## DESTINATION

The signs would be the first thing telling us we were just about there. They would begin in Georgia at some point and continue on huge billboards, telling us how much longer we had to get there. After that, it would feel as though it would be forever until we actually got there. Usually, we would arrive in the afternoon or just around supper time. We'd load all our bags onto one of those hotel luggage carriers and head in. We'd usually need two.

I would always be so ready to jump out of the car and start doing things.

"Come on, Slim! We're here! We'll go to the parks tomorrow." Dad seemed just as excited as I was.

We were officially at Disney World. This was the happiest place in the world to me. It would take a little while to check in and we'd just be standing there, but I'd use this time to check everything out. There'd be Donald Duck shows playing, Mickey faces galore; I was in heaven. As soon as we'd head up to the room and unload the cart with the luggages, Dad would ask if I wanted to come to return them. You bet your ass I wanted to. Mom would stay back in the room and as soon as that door would close and she couldn't see, I'd jump right on the cart and Dad would start pushing me faster and faster down the halls. I don't know why, but it was always so much fun to race in hotel hallways.

My mom was always in charge of putting together the itinerary. At one time, she had us going to breakfast, lunch, and dinner every single day that we visited. It may not seem like a lot, but if you consider the time it took to go to the park, be seated and eat our food...it would take up most of our time each day instead of focusing on going on the rides among other things.

I could write a whole book about all our trips, but I will select a few memorable times that we went.

Of course, when you're a child, you've gotta get the characters' autographs. Scratch that, you don't even have to be a child for this. But anyway, we all walked into the Magic Kingdom, and we were scheduled to eat at the Crystal Palace. Winnie the Pooh and friends are there. All the characters usually circulate the room and make their way to each table. The big, puffy pink head came bobbing from around the corner, and that's when we realized I had forgotten my autograph book.

"Oh no," I said and looked down, upset. Dad was already up and out of his seat, ready to go purchase a new one when...

"Don't worry, Joe. Let's just use this napkin. I've got a pen," Mom suggested. Dad's and my jaw both dropped, as if to say "Really...?" It was too late for us to debate with the idea as Piglet had just arrived at our table. He patted me on the head and did several different poses as Dad took a picture of us. Just as he was about to leave, Mom called over, "Wait!" and handed him a napkin with the pen.

You won't even guess what he did next...

Piglet looked down at the items laid out before him and shook his head and walked away. HE WALKED AWAY!

My dad's face was bright red as I struggled to gulp down my drink instead of spitting it out.

"Who pisses off Piglet?!" he asked through his stifled laughs.

"I was just trying to help!" Mom retorted, as she seemed to try to shrink down in her seat.

We did not use napkins for autographs after that. When we left the restaurant eventually and walked around, Mom had to use the restroom.

"Come with me, see if you have to go," she called back to me. She was walking ahead toward the restroom when Dad snuck one of the walkie talkies to me and bent down to whisper in my ear.

"Bring this with you and slip it in her bag without her knowing," he said. I nodded my head because I knew whatever he had planned was going to be good.

When we got in, I managed to slip the walkie talkie in her bag and then she went into one of the stalls. When I went into the one next door and finished, I washed my hands. That's when I heard a very loud sound coming from the stall she was in.

"PFFFFFFFFFFFFFT!!!!!!" A fart echoed through the bathroom. I smiled and looked over at her stall, as everyone else did too. The women in the bathroom started filing out right away.

"YOUR DAD DID THIS DIDN'T HE?!" she yelled from the bathroom. I couldn't stop laughing. I ran out of the bathroom and Dad was bright red outside also laughing hysterically. But the best part was when she came out of the bathroom.

"That wasn't nice!!!" she said and shoved the walkie talkie back at him. We just kept laughing and the more we did, the more mad she got.

There was another crazy journey we went on, but this time it was at a different park. Animal Kingdom. This park was beautiful with all the animals. When I was young, they hadn't had as many rides as they do now.

One of my favorite restaurants out of all the kingdoms was actually Donald's Breakfastsaurus. Mickey Mouse and friends all walked around in their Jurassic Park themed costumes like they were park rangers. We would go there for breakfast (hence the name) and IT WAS A BUFFET! Yes...all you can eat pancakes...eggs...waffles........and especially bacon!

A bright idea popped into my mom's head as we walked through the park. There was a nice, colorful sign that said, "Come join Rafiki's Safari." Neither me nor my dad were enticed by this, but somehow my mom was.

"Let's go, come on!" she said, grabbing my hand. Dad and I looked at one another and shook our heads. I don't know how we came about giving in, but we found ourselves on this safari. Unfortunately, there were no visible animals, and we were taken far away from the main park. We continued this way and that. There were some pretty cool insect exhibits. Our reservation for dinner was coming soon, so we had to get back.

"Ok, this was your great idea. Now get us back," Dad said. Mom's expression was a reply enough to let us know she had absolutely no clue how to get back. Let's just say that Rafiki's Safari turned into Rafiki's Pilgrimage.

I started this off by introducing "the most magical place." And I had always thought it was, but the magic laid within the people I was with, not where I was.

I touched a ribbon within the page to mark the place, feeling good to share this story.

# MARISSA D'ANGELO

# 12

## SCRATCHING THE SURFACE

The happiest memories are what I remember most. That is why it is like a brick wall is up against the bad. Because they are held back and out of reach, but I do sometimes remember bits and pieces. I have also written in many journals over the years, which have helped to keep my memories in some way, too. The best by far were in elementary school. Middle school was a completely different story, though. Around the start, I began to pull away from my friends. Home turned into a different place for me. My parents battled with many issues and fights at home got worse and worse to the point where my mom moved out and into a rental with my grandma. I stayed with my dad. At this time, I resented my mom because I felt like the medication was more important than me to her. I was just in middle school, so I didn't know much about this.

Before Mom moved out, I remember she asked me to go to the store with her. I took an extra few minutes because I was on AIM (AOL Instant Messenger), talking to my friends. This was an online app on the computer before texting was a common thing. Max was probably the first "boyfriend" I ever had. I put that in quotes because we were likely the most shy people in school and when our friends had found out that we liked each other, they would try to set us up...only for us to just look awkwardly at one another as our cheeks grew bright red. Anyway, I did talk with him quite a lot on AIM. In hindsight, we barely talked about much, mainly music and how he played the guitar. I quickly told him I would be right back and was looking forward to coming back to talk with him.

**Marissa: Hey, I'll brb. Mom wants to go to the store.**
**Max: Ok bye ttyl**

"Come on, Marissa" Mom yelled up. I hopped down each step and went outside. I usually sat in the back right side of the car. I could still see her this way and look out. Mom did her makeup as she drove back then. Not sure how, but she would have the rearview mirror pointing toward her instead of the road behind. We were just heading out to Walmart, which was only five or so minutes away. When we pulled out of the street, she seemed a little bit off, but we made the right onto a side road to reach the main road that brought us to Walmart. I must have looked down for one second and felt my body get pushed forward in my seat. My head hit the back of the right passenger seat and I felt very dizzy all of a sudden. Out of the corner of my eye, I could see a piece of metal from the car rolling down the hill. The impact of metal on metal made a loud screeching sound while the car we were in continued down the hill we were on. Mom was ok, the damage was on my side of the car. Nonno came because he was closer to us than Dad was. When he came, he put his hands on his hips in disbelief that she ran into a parked car.

"You ok, Rissa?" he asked as soon as he got there. I

nodded my head. At least that motion still worked in my neck, although it felt stiff. Nonno drove me home because we were close by to the house. I got back on the computer as I had promised.

> **Marissa:** Hey, I just got in a car accident
> **Max:** OMG r u ok?
> **Marissa:** Yeah, my head hurts so I'm gonna lie down
> **Max:** Ok ttyl feel better

When my dad came home from work, he was livid. Not only was the car totaled, but I was involved in this, too. He ended up bringing me to an orthopedic for my neck to get checked out. I had whiplash.

I put my pen down from writing. This memory wasn't terrible at all compared to other things that went on, but baby steps…

Cece noticed I was done writing for the time being.

"How does that feel?" she asked.

I was honest. "Like I didn't even scratch the surface of my past." It was going to take time to do this.

"You will," she said. "Next week?"

"Next week."

# MARISSA D'ANGELO

# 13
## CONFUSION

The following week seemed bare. There was just something missing. Well, everything was missing. I felt like I couldn't truly move on until I took that brick wall down. There were so many things to say. I found myself spending much of my time writing, so even though I wasn't at therapy, I continued in my own notebook.

As I grew older, whatever my parents were doing seemed to have more and more of an effect on them. It seemed to happen the most when it was late at night and I wasn't even clear why. When I got out of school, my mom helped me with my homework and before I knew it, the night had already come upon us and it was time for me to go to bed. Before I went, I remember my dad coming to tuck me in.

He pushed in each side of the blanket so it was snug against me.

"There, now you're as snug as a hot dog," he had said. "Do you think you can tuck me in, too?" he joked.

"I'll be sleeping!" I said back. He reached over and kissed my forehead, then headed out. He flicked off the hallway light outside my room.

"Hey Dad, can you leave the hallway light on?" I asked,

hoping he heard me. In an instant, the hallway outside my room was illuminated in light.

"Goodnight, Dad. I love you."

"I love you too, Slim. 100." I closed my eyes and before I knew it, I was asleep.

"Get out of my house!!!" Dad yelled from downstairs.

"Shh, You'll wake her," she called back. I jumped out of bed and rushed down the stairs.

"What's going on?" I asked, rubbing my eyes. The two of them were in the kitchen. Dad's face was bright red and Mom looked very tired.

"Oh, you want to know what happened? Well, your mother stole something of mine," Dad said.

"I didn't take anything. I don't know what you're talking about!" she pleaded. It went back and forth for a while. I was too young at that point to know what they were talking about exactly, but I just simply made a suggestion "Just give back whatever it was, it's ok. Or we can go to the store and get something else and replace it?" I said. This should've closed the case. All set...right?

"No, this is something I can't get back. I know you took it," Dad said. He was seeing red and there was no reasoning with him at this point. I got all worked up and just begged both of them to stop, but that didn't seem to matter. They were both yelling and screaming back and forth at one another. The time on the stove read 3:05 a.m. I had school the next day. At some point, they left the room that they had been in and gave one another space. That's when I was able to finally get back to bed.

I wasn't able to recall much else of what happened, but I do remember the puzzle pieces eventually aligning. The medication started to have a huge impact on my family.

# 14

## THAT SOMEONE

I was taking a lazy day, which was unusual for me. I decided to turn on the TV and go through the many different streaming platforms to find a show. Law & Order was always a solid pick and easy to interest me, no matter the episode. At first, my dog squeaked her toy repeatedly and pressed it against my face.

"Drop it," I said, firmly. She refused and continued to press it into my face. I then decided to hide under the blanket, but still was met with constant pushing. One of the best things is to redirect the dog toward something else, so I sat myself up and let the blanket fall to my feet as I looked for a bone she could chew on. I pretended to chew on it, "Num, Num, Num" to try to gain her interest in that over the toy that she had. She immediately pounced right away to where I sat and snatched the bone out of my hands, heading over to the end of the couch to gnaw on it.

I took a sigh of relief that I could finally rest now that she was occupied, so I continued the show. This episode started a little bit different than the others as Olivia (the main character who is a Special Victims Unit police officer) was visiting a friend and just so happened to walk into a burglary turned bad. As soon as she walked in, one of the men slammed the door shut quickly and put his gun up to her head, grabbing her. She had revealed that she was a police officer and while the other robbers grew intimidated, the one that had the gun to her head asked her where her weapon was so he could remove it and took her phone. She cooperated, but they soon took them upstairs to a bedroom where they had tied up a little boy's hands to a railing of some sort in the room so he couldn't leave. They did the same with Olivia and the little boy's older sister was taken into another room with the lead robber. Olivia and the little boy could hear the girl's screams as the boy begged to be freed so he could help his sister because he couldn't bear to hear her screams. At this point, I had to pause the episode and collect myself. I began writing.

A memory that I had buried so deep down was opened up and now was as if it was a fresh wound once again. In sophomore year of high school, I wanted to be accepted so bad, which I am sure everyone does—that is normal. I would see everyone else in relationships and they looked so happy, and I just wanted this. I remember being bored out of my mind in my bedroom one night while my parents were likely watching television or something. They still had their prescription medication problem, so they were probably passed out downstairs. Anyway, my computer made a sound, and I saw I had a message on Facebook from a boy named Rob. It was a simple, "hey," but prior to responding, I had to figure out who this boy was and how he knew me. I began my investigation.

In his first profile picture, Rob had a Santa hat on and looked like a goofball, with a smile from ear to ear and very white teeth. He had a small nose that looked a little flattened, but his eyes were mesmerizing. They were a light blue that truly offset the rest of his dark features. His short, dark hair was curly, and he had very dark eyebrows that made his eyes stand out all the more. I was immediately interested. I clicked out of his photo and scrolled down to see our mutual friends. We had a few, that was ok. I made a mental note in my head to contact one of those mutual friends that I knew so I could ask them about him.

I began to type back. "Hey, who are you?" I said.

Instantly, he responded. "Well, I'm Rob. Who are you?" he joked back. It was an obvious question because you could see our names right there on our profiles, but I more so meant to ask him to tell me about himself.

"Well, I'm Marissa! I meant, tell me about yourself," I replied.

"Oh ok. I like to surf and go outside a lot. I think you're really pretty, so I wanted to talk to you."

From that point on, we just about talked all the time. Whenever I saw he had sent me a message, my stomach would flutter with butterflies in it. We both shared a lot of the same interests. He loved '80s music as I did too. He was also very funny and could make me laugh no matter what. When my parents would be arguing, he could still make me smile. He turned into an escape for me from my dysfunctional home life. I drew a portrait of him too. I remember how good he made me feel and gave me the motivation to draw and write more often.

After weeks of talking, we decided to meet at an outdoor mall. We both did not have our licenses still, so his dad had dropped him off there while my mom came along because she didn't trust just dropping me off. He was such a goof, and we were constantly talking still as we walked around. I remember when we went to the candy store; he wanted to steal something, but I had to beg him not to. I was blind to his true nature. He went on vacation to Florida and told me how he was surfing and wrote Marissa's on his belly in a sharpie so no girls would hit on him. He was so silly like that. I loved it. He later came back from vacation, and I invited him over to my house to hang with me and my family. Right before he came over, I remember looking at myself in the mirror. I would normally put in hair extensions and a lot of makeup, but this time I truly felt loved for me, so I did not do any of that. When he came over, he tried talking to my dad, but he was sleeping, and we couldn't really wake him up. I was very sad about this because I wanted Rob to meet him. My mom got my dad to go upstairs and lay down in his bed, then she went outside to garden. She suggested we go for a walk around the neighborhood. There was a stream that was really beautiful in the woods across from my house. I wanted to show it to him because it was a special place for me. A place I would come when I had no one to talk to.

There was a bit of a steep hill on the way down to the stream and we held onto one another as we made our way down. This was honestly a bad idea because if he went down, so did I, and vice versa. Luckily, we did not go tumbling. We sat down near the stream and started kissing a little. He reached his hand under my skirt, and I told him not to, pushing his hand away. We continued kissing, and he pushed me down toward the ground. He didn't touch under my skirt again, but we just kept kissing. It felt really good to kiss him, as I had not really done that before. We stopped for a bit and I just closed my eyes and lay there, peaceful. When I opened my eyes again, I saw he had his pants down a bit.

I started freaking out right away. "I can't. I've never done this before. I don't want to. I'm not even protected. I don't want to, please," I said, again and again being put in a very uncomfortable situation.

He smiled and calmly said, "Ok, that's fine. We can wait for when you are ready." Then he kissed me again, pushing me down to the ground, and I felt his hand push something under my skirt and felt something I had never felt before. I blacked out what happened next, but I know we had sex. I remember it hurt me a lot, but I think it was too painful of an experience to face. He did what he did, and we walked back and that was the last time I saw him. I could have told my father right away when I got back or even my mother, but I didn't because I didn't want to cause them pain. I knew if I kept it to myself it wouldn't cause them pain. As for my dad, he wouldn't have left it to the police to solve and he would have personally hunted down Rob and killed him. That would've meant I would've lost my dad. I didn't want to lose my dad. So, I decided not to tell either of them. Rob hadn't messaged me, but I was a nervous wreck as I wasn't on protection, so I had to have my friend purchase Plan B for me, which is the morning-after pill to prevent pregnancy. A few days of no contact and Rob had sent me a long message on Facebook about how he didn't wanna settle for me and how he wanted to have time to go party and do things. I was torn up emotionally and physically. I didn't know what to say or do. I was violated. In my mind, I told myself it was definitely not sexual assault or anything because I would've tried to punch him if it was. And I didn't punch him. I lay there defenseless. I didn't defend myself. Why? I don't know.

Months passed by and I tried to move on with someone else but was met with messages late one night from Rob saying exactly this: "I see you're with someone now. No matter how hard you try, you will never get back what I took." I felt like someone had just stabbed me straight through the heart. At that point, I blocked him. He seemed to know exactly what he was doing the whole time. To this day, I can't really lie down in small spaces or underneath anything because it is traumatizing and reopens the wound.

I was not able to continue watching that episode and I skipped over it to something else.

# 15

## FAR & FEW BETWEEN

Your true friends are far and few between, but you can count them on just one hand. The rest are acquaintances.

After my encounter with that very tragic nightmare, I had bottled it up and decided it was my fault for not doing anything about it. I started pulling away from a lot of people. I felt embarrassed and ashamed of my life. I thought back to high school. I tried not to associate with people much and just attended classes and looked forward to going home each day. I thought I'd begin writing about the friends that I did talk to.

The main people I spoke to were Ann and Kimberly. Ann introduced me to a couple of new people whom she wanted to sit with for lunch from then on: Kris, Anne, and Braydon. They seemed okay; so, I opened up to them a bit and was friendly. One day, I came into lunch and Kris and Ann were both out of school sick. I said "Hello" to Anne and sat down to eat. I remember Anne saying how fat Kris was, but I said that she was pretty and had really nice hair. The next day, I was out of school. In the afternoon, I got a warning call from Ann. She said not to go anywhere near the usual lunch table because everyone was fuming mad at me. I had no idea what I did, but I took her advice and sat with my other friend Kimberly the next day. I caught a glimpse of the old table I sat at and noticed everyone staring and giving dirty looks. I was scared to get up to get food because I thought they'd humiliate me and I did not know what was next. So, I asked Kimberly to, but she just said that she would go with me. It turns out that Kris ended up being right in front of me. I heard her talking to her friends about me, calling me very mean names. She said that she would squash me. I went back to the table with Kimberly and felt something hit the side of my head as I was trying so hard to keep my focus on the opposite side of the cafeteria. But then there were even more little pieces of food being chucked my way. Some landed directly on my plate of food that I hadn't touched; I had no appetite. So that was the last straw. I decided I would try to confront her like an adult and boy, was I wrong.

I walked right over to her table. "I did not call you any names. Please, just stop. Don't you see that these are all rumors that people are lying to you?" It was honestly the strangest thing ever, because the people who she thought were CLOSEST to her were the ones speaking behind her back. She was so angry that her face was bright red, and she was yelling at me with different profanities as spit was coming out of her mouth and onto my face. I remember I kept asking what I did wrong because I honestly had no idea. I finally broke down and didn't want to show anyone I was crying, so I ran out of the cafeteria and collapsed beside a wall in the hallway and bawled my eyes out. All the memories of my past came flooding through my mind along with the Kris incident that was currently happening. I felt weak and out of control. Memories of my parents' drug addiction, Rob & everything was flooding in. I also thought about not being able to talk to my mom because she was in and out of rehab to try to get better.

I remember Kimberly came right next to me to console me. My current boyfriend Matt walked right by me, and Kimberly yelled at him for not even thinking to comfort me. Sometimes I feel everyone was in on this. I ended up going home and found out I still couldn't escape the threats, as Kris was even emailing me, yelling and screaming. I defended myself to her because I didn't feel it was right not to. I even remember saying how she lost a real good friend for a stupid reason. She came out with the fact that I apparently called her fat and so I got so angry that I tried and tried to reason with her and got nowhere. I burst through from holding back and said, "Fine, if you want to think that I said you are fat, then go right ahead. You're fat. Happy? 'Cause apparently even when I didn't call you that, I am doomed either way." I brought the emails with me to the principal's office so Kris would leave me alone. The principal said she couldn't do anything because I defended myself and spoke back. She did send a letter home, though.

After all this, I ended up breaking up with Matt and he went out with Anne, the girl who had set me up to Kris. They eventually broke up, but years later, Matt had begged my forgiveness. I did forgive him, but did not go back out with him. I learned the painful lesson of not making the same mistake twice. I feel the best revenge I could have gotten was being successful in life. I still feel removed from my past, as if it did not happen at all. I think I subconsciously formed a shield to block away the pain.

# MARISSA D'ANGELO

# 16
## SENIOR YEAR

I kept avoiding therapy. I wrote enough about the times in my life and no longer wanted to focus on what was going on for me. I began to draw my attention elsewhere and instead of helping myself, I helped others. When I couldn't make any more excuses to not come to therapy, I pushed myself to go and took out my notebook to write while I waited in the lobby.

By this time, I had moved to another town and had to start my senior year at a whole other high school. I lived with my mother then and it broke my heart to put that distance between myself and my father, but as the years went on, it just got worse and worse. At the end of my junior year, I had an emotional breakdown. I don't remember much from it, but what I do know is that I was not able to be in school because I had been found with slits on my wrists. I was pushed to see a therapist at a clinic and my mom ended up losing her job because she was forced to call out of work each day so she could be with me. I was not allowed to be alone at this time. What kills me is I bet my parents thought the blame was all on them, but it truly wasn't. It was a mix of everything, including the bullying incidents, Rob, and family problems. It is not as black and white as people try to make it. So, I ended up just staying at my mom's and she was doing well during this time, actually.

When I first walked into the new school that I would attend my final year, I was immediately overwhelmed and intimidated. Compared to my previous school and town, it was massive and had a total of four floors while the last one only had two. It was likely quadruple the size of my last school. I sucked in my tears while I met with the guidance counselor and my mother. We had put together a schedule for my upcoming year.

The guidance counselor was fairly helpful in determining what classes I needed in order to graduate. She was in her rolling chair on the other side of her desk and clicking away like a madwoman on her computer. Her thick, black hair came down to her shoulders, and she wore a blazer and looked as if she was just another office worker. I found out a biology class I took at my other school had to be redone so, unfortunately, I would be with freshman, but I didn't mind that. Whatever it took.

"You need to pick some elective courses. Anything you like?" she asked, not looking away from her computer. I looked down for a minute at my feet and I was surprised my mom didn't answer for me. I couldn't seem to think of anything, but then an idea popped into my head.

"Well, I like cooking."

"Perfect! We have a school restaurant here, but it would start at 8 a.m. You would work there before school by serving breakfast to teachers and other students and then learn the ropes of the kitchen with Mr. Green," she said, seeming to be done with the computer now as she looked over at me.

The early time made me shudder a bit, but I recollected

myself and thanked her before leaving. As soon as I got into my mom's car in the parking lot, the tears came crashing down.

"What's the matter? I thought that went well!" mom asked.

"I miss my dad and I don't want to be at a new school," I said, frantic.

"Well, you'll see him soon. It's ok, it's just for one year that's all. You couldn't go to the other school because we don't live in that town anymore. Just one year, that's all. It'll go by," she said.

The tears just continued coming down and as we pulled out of the parking lot and onto the main road, I turned back to look at the school again. It only made me feel worse. I would be starting here in just a few days.

A few months went by and I was able to face the school on my own, without any friends or anyone I knew. Just alone. I walked right past people and did not plan on making any friends, either.

Each morning, I woke up bright and early to work in the restaurant. When I came in sometimes, I would try to reach my apron and, because the others were much taller and Mr. Green was incredibly tall, the hook was up very high. He had short, red hair and wore his chef coat at all times. In fact, I honestly don't remember anytime I saw him without that coat on.

"Need some help there, champ?" he said as he took the top apron off the hook and handed it over to me. I smiled nervously and nodded my head. "You're on pancakes today. Get ready." Before we took our coursework and learned different techniques about cooking and baking, we all split up jobs in the back of the kitchen to serve breakfast. There were several stations that we rotated through: Omelet, Pancake/French Toast, Breakfast Sandwich, Fryolator, Cash Register, and Coffee. My least favorites were Coffee and Omelet. With coffee, students but teachers mostly would get very anxious as they were ordering, and I just never seemed to do it right. Omelets always stuck to the pan for me and when I went to flip them, some of the omelet would end up on the floor. This school that I was in comprised a very diverse population. There were many lower-economic status populations, and the restaurant was an initiative to get young adults trained so they were ready to join the working class out of high school if they couldn't afford to attend a college or their grades slacked so they didn't get accepted to any. In the restaurant class, I was the only female. I still didn't mind it. And it was always good listening to the guys goof around with one another. They all left me alone and helped me whenever I need it, so it was nice.

By the end of the year, the students in the class that had the highest grade were elected to take the ServSafe Sanitation Exam for free. This is a certification that will allow you to be a manager at a restaurant and definitely sought out for. I remember studying for this like crazy as I made more than 200 flash cards. There were questions about cross-contamination, food safety, sanitizing, equipment, you name it. I believe there were three kids in the class that were chosen to take this exam and I was one of them, so I did not want to let Mr. Green down. He had been a great mentor to me. After spending many nights studying the flashcards I made, I took the exam and passed it. In my head, I planned to go to culinary school straight out of high school.

One day as I was leaving the restaurant to attend another class, Mr. Green said he would write me a late pass to my next class but would like to see me in his office. I had never been that far back in the kitchen to even notice he had a small office on the side. The door was usually closed, but this time I could see piles and piles of binders and books all over the place. His desk had a whole mess of items all over, in no particular order.

"Is everything ok?" I asked, confused.

"What do you want to do after high school? Have you started to apply yet?" he asked.

"I want to go to Johnson & Whales for Culinary & Baking and Pastry," I proudly said. My over-confidence was met with a drawn look on his face, as if he was going to break some terrible news to me.

"I've been working with you all year and I see you have a lot of potential. You can do that if you want to, but I see that you have so much drive in you to do a lot more in this world. I went into culinary because I was not good at much else. You have a lot of other things you are good at. I think you should recalculate that decision," he said.

I didn't really know what to say at first. In a way, this honesty was very nice, and he did fit in many compliments, but also crushed the dreams I had inadvertently.

"Thank you, Mr. Green. I'll think about it. I'm not sure what else I would do, but I'll think about it," I said.

"Yeah, you got it. And I wrote the letter of recommendation for you to go to college. Here you go," he said and handed it to me. Attached was his card, too. "My card is on there if you ever need anything or want to talk, too. You're going to do great things, kid."

I left his office feeling warmth inside my chest, but at the same time felt a little defeated. I believed him. I could always do culinary and baking on the side, but what else would I do? What career path would I go down in college?

One of the elective classes I had signed up for was Personal Finances. It was in the computer lab and comprised a very small class. I and another girl were the only two girls in the class, well besides the teacher. On the first day, we were given a syllabus of some sort explaining what would be on the final exam at the end of the course. There was some down time to explore different websites and banking options. I don't remember much from this class other than the friend I made and a kid that was very much into My Little Pony (he was about 17 years old...to each their own, I guess).

I had been taking notes in the syllabus that I planned to use to study for the final exam when the boy that had originally sat diagonal from me moved to sit right next to me. He immediately took an interest in me; why, I do not know.

"Hey, where are you from?" he said in a friendly voice.

"Oh, I'm from this small town over near New Haven." I continued typing away at my computer.

"Is this your first year here? Haven't seen you before," he said. I looked over at him for a moment, noticing he had dark brown eyes and wore glasses. He also had fairly short hair and latte-brown skin. He wore all black, which was typical for a lot of teenagers in certain groups.

"Yeah." I kinda wanted to close the conversation and not carry on any longer, so I purposely made it one-sided.

The next day, he handed me a paper that had Sharpie all over it in some kind of weird design that took me a minute to recognize the design comprised my name.

"Wow, thank you. Do you like art?" I asked. I was actually quite impressed, but still disinterested. Maybe he could be a friend?

"Oh, it's just something I do for fun. Yeah, I like to sketch. I'm taking an art class for my other elective," he said.

"That's cool. I'm in the ceramics class, so I'm also doing some art. I'm making a Pinocchio right now," I said, thinking about the friends I had made in that class, too.

"Nice. We should share some of our art someday That would be cool." I nodded. We continued to sit next to one another for the rest of that semester's class. Toward the end of the year, we would frequently pass one another in the halls and show pictures of the things we had made. He did end up becoming a good friend to me.

The biology class I had to take with freshman was brutal, but fairly easy as long as I kept up. My teacher went to Virginia Technical School and was actually attending when there was the school shooter many years before. I felt a connection to her immediately because she had been through deep trauma too.

The first day I came in, I elected to sit at the very back of the class. I was pretty embarrassed to be the only senior in this class. There were no desks; instead, there were long black tables to do science experiments on in groups. Two chairs were placed at each long table. I was early to class, but after just a few minutes, there was a boy that sat next to me and another right in front who was on the basketball team. To his right was a girl with dark brown hair, much like mine. The boy to my left had very light skin; actually, whiter than me. His face was painted in freckles, and he had blue eyes. His hair was very light but had a reddish tone to it.

"Hey girl, heyyyyy" he said, obnoxiously. I put my left hand up to the side of my face to block him out of my sight.

"What's your name?" he asked. Again, I ignored him. The "Hey girl, hey" was enough for me to know he was looking for something I had no interest in. The basketball player in front of me turned around and just said, "Dude, don't think she's interested. Shut up." He turned around after looking at me.

The teacher came on over and saved me from having to deal with any more, thank goodness. She, too, had an entire syllabus made up for each of us that we were to follow in depth. We ended up learning about anatomy and also some different diseases that were easily transmittable. The boy next to me turned out to be a harmless goofball, and I did end up saying hello to him, but not much. We worked together with the basketball player and girl with brown hair on many projects throughout the class. At the very end of the year, we had independent projects that we had to present to one another. I forget what mine was about, but I remember using a poster board at home and putting a lot of effort into it. When I presented it, I had one question at the end.

"Are you going to be a teacher?" one of my peers asked.

"What, why?" I said. This had nothing to do with my

actual project, so I was stumped.

"You're really good at presenting. I think you would be a great teacher," he said. I saw the other kids nodding their heads in the room. They clapped and then I, bright red in the face, walked back to my desk in the back of the room. This sparked a thought in my head, though, a thought I would carry with me for a very long time.

Toward the end of my senior year, I looked at just a few different colleges. Quinnipiac University, Southern Connecticut State University and Western Connecticut State University were mainly it. I wanted to stay local.

When I first went to Quinnipiac University, I was dead set on going as soon as I stepped foot on their campus. They had gorgeous views, being right next to Sleeping Giant Mountain and their dining hall was massive, along with their library. Everything was kept so clean, and I remember telling my mom I wanted to go there. Then, we got to billing. I planned to be a teacher. I knew it would be very difficult for me to pay off a debt if I had to take out so many student loans. On to the next, unfortunately, which was Western Connecticut State University. It was cute. It reminded me of the third pig's house in The Three Little Pigs because the dorms and most campus buildings were constructed entirely of brick. Last place was Southern Connecticut State University, which was only ten or so minutes away from my parents'. Despite the history, I wanted to be close to them. No one is perfect, and they raised me. As soon as I started on their tour, it felt like home instantly. It was right in the inner city, but felt otherwise as it was set aside in a grassy area and once you were on campus, there was a huge middle courtyard between the arts building and student center. Some students were walking to their classes and used that courtyard to cross campus.

When the tour group went to the student center, which was the newest building at the time, we had to cross a bridge. I remember I looked over the bridge and saw the blue owl mascot riding in a golf cart to get to wherever he was going. It was the funniest thing. There were several floors to the student center. On the lowest level (below the bridge, but next to a small parking lot), there was a campus bookstore where I proudly purchased an owl plushie that sported an SCSU sweatshirt. He joins me in my classroom when I teach. The first level held the food court. There was a pizza/Italian place, Mexican food, subs and a Dunkin' Donuts that I was a frequent customer at. We walked back over the bridge toward "Conn Hall" and entered. The lower level didn't hold much, but you walked around and went up the stairs and then you were in heaven. But I'm not even at the best part yet. Early in the mornings, an omelet chef would make omelets that were made to order just for you. Yes, I was one of those that woke up around six just for that yummy omelet. Past that, there was a stir fry station. A cook stood behind it and you could request different items in your stir fry. Then, there was a buffet style area with common finger foods like chicken fingers, fries, et cetera. Toward the end, there was heaven...Cookie and dessert heaven. Dozens and dozens of cookies were encased here. No wonder "Freshman fifteen" was a thing. It was so hard to walk away during the tour, but I made a mental note to come back here often. After that, we visited the library and dorm halls. I got all the information I could and decided on Southern. I chose to be close to home so that, in case anything happened, I would be near enough to go help if it was needed. This was a weird time because I just got into a relationship recently and the boy and his family were very great and loving. They were supportive. I found myself spending a lot of my time over there. And they, too, were about ten minutes away from Southern, if not closer. It was going to be a good time!

I reminisced about these times while waiting outside Cece's office. After a few minutes, she came out the front door instead of her office. Her hair was disheveled, and she looked as though she was in a hurry. She acknowledged me as she made her way toward her office and fumbled for the key.

"I'm so sorry! I taught a class at a college today and traffic was backed up bad. You weren't waiting long, were you?"

"No, not at all!" I said, getting up to hold the door for her after she opened it. "I could give you a minute if you need one?"

"You're ok, come right in!" she said as she walked in and piled her books on top of the countertop in back. I could hear her as she exhaled, as if she were relieved to be free of the books and had carried them a long way. I sat down and picked up the pencil, but then dropped it down and looked blankly at the desk.

"What's going on?" she asked, startled, since every other time I wrote until my fingers were red.

"I don't know where to begin. There's not much to tell, yet there's so much, if that makes any sense?" I started to explain more, which I often did when I got nervous. "There's a lot that's happened, but it's difficult to find the words."

# MARISSA D'ANGELO

# 17
## MISSED CALLS

The day started like any other. I walked over to my work right after school usually, but I had just graduated a few weeks before. A few months before, I was getting fitted for a black and white dress at a dry cleaner. I had gone with my grandma. Dresses and pretty much everything was long on me because of my height. The lady behind the counter was very nice but didn't talk much. She had short black hair that came down to her ears and dressed very neatly. Not one thing out of place about her outfit. She was Korean, and I later came to find out, she visited over there quite often. I had told her I needed to get something hemmed, and she sent me back to the changing room while I left Grandma in the front.

I guess she put in some good words about me. I remember coming out of the fitting room and the lady, Lilah, asked, "You wanna start work here?"

I glanced at Grandma, and she was just smiling from ear to ear innocently. What had she been saying? I turned my attention back to Lilah.

"I'd love to." I was looking for a job for a few months then and really wanted to save up as much money as I could so this was great, but I was so nervous as to what to expect from working at a dry cleaner. This must've been the first time I honestly stepped foot in a dry cleaner. I held up each side of my dress and walked over to the mirror and so the seamstress could measure the length.

Fast forward about one year. I worked there so often that I began to handle the store completely alone. There were several tasks at the dry cleaners, but fortunately no cleaning was done on premises, and everything was sent out otherwise it would've been a sauna in there. My main job was to intake clothes and tag them along with helping customers by handing them their pickup orders.

On June 5, 2012, it was my dad's birthday, just like any other year. I planned to head there as soon as work was done. I headed in and relieved Jim, the owner of the dry cleaners, of his shift. As soon as he left and it was slow, I called my dad. It went right to voice mail. I called mom. No answer. My mind wandered. Were they hurt? Dead? What happened? A customer parked right in front of the store. I had to pull myself together. It was fine. All would be well.

The customer had light brown hair and was an older gentleman. He wore glasses, but I knew him when I saw his Volvo pulling in. I had already typed his name in the computer and was fetching his clothes. They were on the rack, waiting for him as soon as he made his way to the register.

"Wow, you're good!" he said. "Every time. How's school going for you?"

"I am done! I start SCSU in the fall!" I smiled. He handed me the card, and I quickly put it in the computer. I wanted to get him out so I could try calling my parents again.

He waved and took his clothes out. I hadn't even waited for him to step out of the door before dialing mom. Sometimes, she would answer more because dad didn't always have his ringer on. He was like me in that he didn't have sound on his phone unless he forgot. I'm not sure why he did it, but I would keep mine off since I was working. It was only four-thirty at that moment. I just wanted to leave work so I could drive to my dad's and check on them. But I couldn't. I had to wait till seven. There was no one to cover for me.

I decided to clean at work and just told myself they were at home sleeping. That's all. Just sleeping. Except, I knew deep down something was very, very wrong. I vacuumed the entire store in between customers and then mopped. It was around six forty-five before I knew it, but time was still dragging. I started closing procedures far too early and was just waiting. The last thing I had to do was cash out the register. At six fifty-eight, I thought I could get away with it and walked over to the front to lock the door and turn the sign off. The parking lot was empty on one side. There were just a few cars on the other side where Starbucks was.

I had just finished counting all the ones when I heard a knock on the door.

"Ugh, don't even!" I muttered under my breath. It was too late to hide too, because she had definitely seen me. Looking up from the register, I could see a woman with two large laundry bags in her arms as she knocked at the door again. I reluctantly let her in.

"So sorry! Just got out of work and made it!" she declared

on her way in. By the time I made her invoice and sent her on her way, it was already 7:06. This time, I turned the light off in the store and quickly scrambled to tag all of her items.

Seven thirty-two. Damn. I gathered my bag and called both numbers again on the way to the car. Something was definitely not right. I headed over to my dad's. My mom's car wasn't there when I arrived. I knocked at the front door and even the back. I walked around toward the front again and started banging on the window to the TV room where they usually were.

Come on, please be ok. I went over to the garage door and pushed it up since it was usually open. Dad's radio was playing '80s music in the garage, as always. When I walked into the TV room, it was on, but no one was inside. I checked in at each room in the house, yelling, "Mom...Dad..." but there was no answer. I called my dad's parents.

"Hello? Rissa?" Nonno answered, as if he expected my call.

"Hey Nonno, have you heard from my parents?"

"Yes, Rissa. I was waiting till you were out of work. They got in an accident with a tractor trailer."

My heart stopped right there.

"Oh, please tell me they're ok."

"They are ok. Just a little banged up. They're at the hospital now," he said.

I was so grateful that they made it. But I had no idea what would be in store for the next few years. As my family life dwindled down, I started pouring myself more and more into college and reading books.

# 18

# DISASTER

After my parents' accident, things were never the same. It was more chaotic than it had ever been. They were both severely injured from the accident, but my dad sustained worse injuries because he had been thrown into the windshield and a piece of his scalp was on the windshield from the accident. They had just bought KFC and I guess he was eating it, but then it went everywhere. They were driving around a corner when a tractor trailer went over the line and into their car. Every morning and night were a struggle for me, and I know for them, too. Having been concussed and also suffering other impacts, they went to doctors and were prescribed more and more medication to help them with their pain. Unfortunately, the more they were prescribed, the more tolerance they had. Which meant that these medications weren't as effective. In the morning, I would wake up to my mother and father arguing. Sometimes it would even be at all hours of the night. At times, I was pulled in the middle of it and I tried to settle their argument. I was juggling so much. The side effects from the medication that my parents were taking caused them to be very drowsy and a lot of times, they would be sleeping their days away. From the moment that I woke up to the moment I went to sleep, I could feel my heart racing in my chest. Even when I was at work or left them alone at any point, I had no idea what would happen.

*January 27, 2017*

*My heart is breaking. My dad is in the hospital because of the medication. I don't know what to do. I don't want to lose him. I'm so scared. Is death just a black, endless screen? Your brain is just off? You can't do anything any longer? If I died, I would like my heaven to always consist of the season of fall. And I would like there to be no buildings or anything man-made. Just trees and leaves.*

*February 12, 2017*

*I know God just wants what is best for me. I know that whatever is meant to be, will be. So, I need to leave it all in God's hands now.*

A few days later, disaster hit. Complete and utter disaster surrounded me and everything I knew. Since my mom and dad were fighting so much and it was mostly about medication, the cops were eventually called. I missed both his and my mom's calls while I was at work because I can't have my phone out while at work. So, I couldn't even help at all when it was going down.

When I went home, neither of them answered. I had no idea what was even going on. I decided to lie down and just cry. My best friend, Nick, was calling me over and over. I didn't answer. He ended up showing up at my place and put on games to play with me. It was nice because I would've been sitting in complete darkness otherwise. When I was left alone, it wasn't good. At this point, my mom's side of the family was involved and so was my dad's. They had been thinking I knew what was going on at the house when I didn't. I had moved out. It was out of my control. I started to question why I even existed. I didn't want to leave, but felt like I only caused problems.

February 14, 2017

Why am I here? I do not belong and I never have belonged. The root of all the problems, even for the problems in my family, is the simple fact that I exist. If I never existed, my parents would not still be creating havoc in one another's lives. I wouldn't be the glue that kept pulling them back together.

I don't want to be here anymore. No one truly cares anyway. I just don't want to be here. I used to think I had a chance. I used to be hopeful for a better tomorrow, but now I realize the truth about it all. If I was no longer here, it would solve everything. I can't think of hurting myself, but I would much rather have that physical pain than emotional. Physical pain can be seen more often, and I can bandage it or go to physical therapy. I can see it and I can heal, or at least let it become a scar. I can't bear the emotional pain and the sad truth that I am all alone in this. If I am being given just one life and if it is going to be like this, then why didn't You take me when I had Kawasaki syndrome as a kid? I was so close to death, and You made me better only to grow up to live in a hell?

I tend to self-blame for everything, even when it had clearly been someone else's doing. I will figure out a way that I am to blame. This is a problem. Shortly after I wrote this, my friends and I went to the movies and spent time together. It helped. I was just attending college and so I decided to take a leap of faith and study abroad.

# MARISSA D'ANGELO

# 19
## ABROAD

Nicaragua or Rome...
As a part of a college requirement, I needed to take a language. Most of my life, I took Spanish. My Nonni Maria's native language was Italian. I thought, how cool would it be if I learned the language and could speak to her in it? She did speak English, but I knew it would give her the best surprise. I signed up. I took the classes for a few years and in my third year, the teacher recommended I go with her on a study abroad-trip to Tuscany. I was very interested, but none of the courses she taught there were required for me. In college, I Majored in Elementary Education, but also Liberal Studies, so I ended up with two degrees. With liberal studies, my concentrations were Anthropology and English Literature. I still needed English courses, so I searched the website. There were opportunities to go to Nicaragua. There, I could learn more about anthropology. This would've been so interesting. I really wanted to go. On the main flyer, there was a rainforest background and a little Capuchin monkey peeking out. It was so cute! But I scrolled down and looked at the courses that would be given and I didn't need any more anthropology courses. I kept going down further.

A statue from Michelangelo and a beautiful historic background were on this flyer. Rome. The courses offered were biblical literature, Roman Literature and the classics. Perfect! These were all English courses and would satisfy the requirements I needed! In my mind, I knew exactly what I was going to do.

Later that night, I went to talk to my dad about it. He got very upset and protective. To say the least, he was shut off to this idea.

"No, that is a bad idea. You don't want to go there," he said without a moment's hesitation. He walked away as if it was decided. Case closed. I followed him.

"Come on, this is a trip with college. It's not by myself!" I protested.

He turned toward me. "You don't want to go over there. It's not safe. Why do you think Nonni moved over here?" he replied.

"It's not safe over in this country either," I muttered, and he couldn't hear. Years later, I figured out he was upset that he wouldn't be able to be close by if something happened. If he were able to go too, then that would have made him feel more at ease. No wonder why he attended almost all the field trips I went on. To be close by if something happened. Mom had just said, "be careful" because she knew I was going to do what I was going to do. I was my father's child, after all.

The next few weeks went by, and I didn't bring it up much more to my dad, but attended several weekly meetings for the trip and signed up. When I told him it was set in stone, he was not happy. I planned to go to Italy to study abroad for four weeks. It was exhilarating. I don't even think either of my parents had stepped outside the country. There were so many things we had planned, along with studying but most of our coursework had to be finished before the trip so we could pair our projects and readings with the real-life thing whether it be a painting, statue, place, church, you name it. The group already met up several times, so we knew one another by now, but the departure to Italy was pretty brutal and long. I tried to sleep, but couldn't because of the adrenaline rush I had. The girl that sat beside me, Coty, told me about how she would normally get very sick on flights. When the attendant came around, she asked us if we wanted a beverage besides water. While I declined, Coty requested wine and showed her ID. I recall questioning that choice in my head given that she would get sick on the plane. But the next thing I knew it, she visited the bathroom and did not come back for a while. She ended up being ok though. When we got off the plane, it was daytime since we had a layover in England. I brought a journal with me to Italy that I tried to write in each day, although it was difficult.

We traveled to Ravenna, which was the first Venice, but due to erosion the water was pushed out and more land formed. Venice and Florence were other places we visited. When you walk out of the train station in Venice, it is a gorgeous site to see the city on water. Of course, my group split the costs to go for a ride in the gondola. The mood was perfect there because even the Italian gondola sailor sang in Italian as we went throughout Venice. Ariccia was another place we visited that a lot of people get married at. It's right on the coast and there are so many beautiful white buildings all around. I pushed a few people to go to Pompeii while the rest of the group took their day off to go to the beach close by to Rome. Pompeii had to have been my favorite place. When I was there, I liked to close my eyes in each place and picture it reconstructed. A lot of the city of Pompeii remained. There were even some bodies of pets and people preserved in place. They had been covered and encased in ash, so you could only see their outline, no small details. But it was so amazing to me that I could see them still to this day. If you looked out from Pompeii, you could see Mount Vesuvius, too. This trip was life changing, and I was so ready to come back and start my life as a teacher.

# 20
## NEW BEGINNINGS

January 19, 2016

Today was my first day of student teaching. Coming into the classroom I was in was like walking into someone else's home: new set of rules, structure, et cetera. The classroom set-up was much different from what I am typically used to seeing. My cooperating teacher used the gradual release model of I do (teacher models), we do (teacher and students do together), you do (students do independently). I enjoyed this a lot, but the teacher and I both agreed on the fact that the students need to learn more independent work skills and strategies in order to be able to work independently. Today, the students continuously needed more guidance through their independent work, even though they had the material modeled for them and worked in groups previously. I noticed one thing I need to work on is my confidence. I'm starting to set some goals and deadlines for myself in the classroom. I want to memorize most of my students' names by Thursday or Friday. By the middle of next week, I want to have led a line of students and instructed a lesson. I really need to see the teacher's plans for lessons during the week and get more involved. Here are some goals I need to work on:

1. Confidence
2. Walk line
3. Teach lesson
4. Memorize Names

Today, I particularly noticed one student who showed he was in the Industry versus Inferiority stage of Erikson's Psychosocial Development Stages. When the student was supposed to be doing "a brief writ,." he instantly showed inferiority. He refused to do anything and hid in his sweatshirt. He felt a sense of incompetence at the moment. In the Industry versus Inferiority stage, the child learns the value of competence. I went over to him and talked him back into working on the assignment. We talked about dogs and he free-wrote about his Pitbull. The students are learning about fraction bars right now, which is great because I just took math for teachers so I can finally use some of what I learned.

January 20, 2016

I was able to check off two items from my goal list! I memorized all my students' names and today's just the second day of school. The kids helped, too. I also walked the students back to their classroom from lunch time. It worked out very well because I am finally grasping my management style. Some teachers bring their students back to the classroom after recess and let them go right in, noisy or not. I had my students wait outside the door in a line and waited until they were quiet. Then, we went in. This helped a lot because the students came in with a better attitude and ready for the next thing. One thing saddened me, but I'm going to learn from it. During writing workshop, one student was sleeping with his head down on his desk. I woke him up and told him to get back to work. Afterward, I spoke to a tutor about it and she explained he has autism and so, he can't do the work since he's not on grade level. I felt very sad, but asked why he wasn't helped on his level so he could progress, and they didn't know. The tutor said some teachers worked with him and helped him to learn to socialize. For example, formulating questions and answers for other people. People take these social nuances and cues for granted. Not everyone gets it as easily. I think the support helps, but he needs more one on one, and it is unacceptable that they let him just sleep the day away. It is doing an injustice for him. It is tough for a classroom teacher because he/she has to help all the students. I need to ask my cooperating teacher what she grades him. I want to know more of what he is already able to do and what he struggles with so that I can continue to help him.

January 26, 2016

Today we went to an assembly. There was a speaker who showed various animals: an iguana, a chinchilla, a boa constrictor, a snake, and a walking stick bug. Also, a frog. It was really cool and good for the students to be exposed to. After the assembly, the classes split up into intervention groups. Students who didn't need intervention logged onto a reading program called Storia on their chrome books. Storia is a personalized website that each student can use that personalizes the online library based on the students' Lexile levels. I think it's very good, but I need to learn more about it. For recess, rules were changed. The teacher said on Tuesdays and Thursdays students would be able to use computers during recess. On Mondays, Wednesdays, and Fridays, students would not be able to use computers and would socialize. Thank the good Lord! They really need more opportunities to socialize. For students who did not understand their homework, she made a small group in the back of the classroom and taught them. She showed them on paper first, then brought their homework out. She also had the two struggling students use a colored pencil to write the correct answers on their homework. When I was walking in the hallway, I ran into the reading specialist and asked her for some more books for the group I usually helped during reading. This group has struggling readers. One girl just came over from Afghanistan and is just learning English. There is another girl who is beginning English too, but she has Cystic Fibrosis and misses a lot of school from being sick often. The boy in my group is the same boy with autism that had usually fallen asleep throughout the day. He reads books really fast, but has difficulty with comprehension. I got the kids two sight word packets and some books.


January 28, 2016

When I came into class, I said good morning to every student and last night, I had pre-sharpened pencils for them so it wouldn't be a problem for them today. Last night, I also drew a picture of Daffy Duck for one of the kids. He begged me to, and I couldn't refuse. He's paying attention very well today, so I think it gave him a boost of motivation that he needed since he has a lot going on at home. I also took it upon myself to collect all the homework and grade it during morning meeting. I bought stickers at the store last night and used them on each homework assignment. It is amazing how difficult kids act when they have more motivation.

I'm really confused as to what is going on though because the students were asked to do one thing 'cause they were done, so I let them. It became an issue because they didn't like the partners I assigned them to. Then, the teacher said they shouldn't have been partners at all. Whoops! Damned if you do, damned if you don't.

The teacher set up a little desk in the back so I can help the three struggling students and I did today. We went over sight words and she has been having a lot of difficulty with the VCE (Vowel + Consonant + E) words like make, cake, ate, et cetera. I need to get a bunch of those words together so she can practice. The subjects are organized for each student by folder. So, for example, reading is the red folder while purple is for writing.

Everyone was rowdy in the room after I helped the students in back, so she had everyone stand up and push in their chairs. Then, they moved around the room as if they were snowflakes. Then, pouring rain. Then, tornadoes. Then, sunny, happy days. When one student was crying because he accidentally got hurt (maybe this was in the tornado part LOL), the teacher told him to get a drink of water and it helped him to calm down.

January 29, 2016

I've made friends with the other third-grade teacher. Before school, she shows me what she's doing with her students. It's cool to see another perspective with the same material. I made myself an answer sheet so I could quickly grade their homework this time. The spelling tests they do here are so interesting. When I was in fourth grade, everyone got the same words on their tests. But with this class, it is different depending on their level. They have a letter names group, within words, et cetera. I like this because it differentiates based on their readiness. It's really, really good. I noticed that the two students who misbehave a lot got perfect scores on their math homework almost every time I graded. Maybe they're bored and misbehave because of that. I really hope those students don't get kicked out because they do have talent. Just behavior issues. But anyway, the teacher gave me some good advice.

- When a student can't focus, sit with them and get them engaged. Leave once they're focused again.

I played Bingo with the students, and it was nice. Some students got an attitude, though. They were mad because they didn't get Bingo.

February 1, 2016

I am going to take attendance the rest of the week and do morning meetings. They do a lot for black history month, which is nice. The teacher had the students who were misbehaving sit right next to her. She also gave a recap of last week. This was very good. Especially after the long weekend.

One student challenged me. He would not listen to me when I told him to sit on the carpet with everyone else. I had to take away a point from him (they use a program called Class Dojo and they can earn or lose points here). He still wouldn't listen. I said he could come back if he stays on the carpet. I ended up sitting down with him and helped him focus. When the students were acting out, the teacher had them all come to the carpet.

In my small reading group, I had the two girls echo read today. It actually helped a lot so I could help the other students. The student who had been falling asleep a lot was given a number line from his special education teacher to help him add and subtract. When I walked around the room while the teacher instructed the students, I tried giving one student a sticker and he flat out said, "No thanks." I guess he's too grown up for this! On our way to lunch one day, two boys got in line next to one another and I guess one was supposed to be in front of the other, but he had stolen his spot...so he ended up putting the other child in a chokehold. These kids are eight to nine years old. Let's just say that I called for assistance right away and they were escorted out by the principal.

February 10, 2016

Today's lesson was a disaster. I felt like crawling in a hole and I still do. But I can only just keep moving on and learn for the future.

February 24, 2016

In our staff meeting today, we were talking about the effectiveness of suspension from school. It is not effective. It is actually a vacation for the students. A reward.

March 7, 2016

Today was insane. One kid pushed another girl into the science experiment buckets. Then, the same kid forcibly pushed another kid into the wall and the kid fell onto his face. The same kid then punched another kid in the face several times.

Holy crap. Please let me help these kids.

# 21

## MORE ABOUT YOURSELF

That day I went back into therapy with Cece and I had a different mindset this time. I didn't have to focus on talking about the bad all the time. For a while, I thought I had little to say besides the bad, but that's only because I was focusing on just that.

"Last time, we talked about the first time you started teaching. Tell me more about yourself again. Let's keep going with that. What did you do after that experience?" she pressed on.

"I decided to go back to school for my master's degree in Special Education. The little boy from my first teaching experience really stayed in my mind and I wanted to learn how to help kids with autism and kids with special needs in general. While I did that, I took a job as a building substitute at the school I worked at. It was frustrating at time because every day I had no idea what position I would be filling. But I got the hang of it after a bit."

"Oh, that's great!" She smiled. I pulled out a journal that I kept from this era and began reading through it.

March 24, 2017

In the morning, I was assigned to a 1<sup>st</sup> grader who normally had a paraprofessional that accompanied him. Previously, I had seen him throw chairs and other objects around the room when he would grow frustrated. We talked about video games because he likes Legos, Minecraft, and grand theft auto (do not ask me why he is allowed to play this game when he is just seven years old). Anyway, he went back to his regular classroom and later on in the day, another paraprofessional told me he had been asking for me and wants me to come back and hang out with him. Is that what he thought this was? It was a good sign, though!

For the rest of the day, I was assigned to a 6th grader who has Asperger's Syndrome. He often yelled at other people and would say "meow" during attendance when his name was called out. I stayed a distance away from him, but helped him when he needed it. While he was at art, I went to bring another 6th grader swimming. She was normally in a self-contained classroom, and I liked to visit with this classroom because they needed a lot of help with their students. I had to help her change for swimming and because I don't have any siblings or anything, it was a bit awkward trying to help her change into other clothes. I almost left her socks on and put the water shoes over them! Maybe I just needed more sleep. After swimming, I had to help her change to regular clothes, and I noticed she had a diaper on so I figured she isn't allowed to be without a diaper but there was no new diaper, so I had to leave the wet one on...and put other clothes over. The whole way back to class she just kept saying "Wet...wet...wet...wet..." and I told the special education teacher what happened, and she said she didn't need the diaper, only for during swimming. I felt so bad! But I guess now I know. I can't even imagine how she must have felt.

After work, I stopped over my dad's, and he isn't mad at me anymore. It's kind of an on and off thing. I went shopping with my friend, Theresa, and I got very pretty dresses. One is pink and goes off my shoulders and I also got a white bathing suit, some earrings, bras, and panties. Very excited to wear the bathing suit and dress!

I ended up coming home and cleaning the whole apartment and a boy I had been talking to apologized to me for being so obsessive about hanging out with me. He is better now though, but I told him I do not feel comfortable jumping into anything which is good. I'll be going to Italy in just two week.s


March 26, 2017

Last night was so much fun! I went dancing at Toad's Place with my friends Mike and Tyler and they are just great people to be around. They were both dancing so silly and it was making me laugh a lot. They were looking for a girl to date and I was supposed to be the "wingman" for them. At one point, I asked Mike where Tyler was and he said, "Looking for a Chiquita," so then I started dancing up toward the stage area. The music was so loud I could feel the vibrations throughout my entire body. It just felt so good. All until a random guy came from behind me and was trying to dance with me. This was the normal thing though, but I just wanted to dance alone. I saw Tyler a few feet away from the stage and gave him a look and mouthed, "Help me!" and he came right over and nudged the other guy away and we went to find Mike. We ended up going back to their dorm with other friends and played Super Smash Bros. and some

Monkey Ball. This was such a great time with friends!

May 28, 2017

   Today, I helped third graders, and then I helped a preschooler with a speech and hearing impairment. I pointed to things like shapes, colors, and body parts and she had to name them. I took down data while she was naming them. She was the cutest little thing! Her long black hair was in a ponytail and she was so eager to learn. She had a bit of a chipmunk voice, too. The day really helped, but I had woken up in the morning shaking because I had a really bad nightmare about my dad. He wasn't himself and was really mad, which the medication seemed to do to him...and I was living back in the house and was trying to sleep, but there was banging from underneath. Constant banging on the ceiling from underneath me. When I asked it to stop, it would only become more and more repetitive.

April 1, 2017

   Ok, so today I will write about the April 1st adventures. I went to see my dad, but he was sleeping so then I went over to my nonni's and we had bread that she made from scratch. It was so good as always. Especially with the ~~jelly~~ butter on it. (I wrote jelly because I'm thinking of having jelly on it in the morning for breakfast). Then, I went home and cleaned and just pretty much worked on college stuff.

April 3, 2017

My dad wasn't in a good mood today. Since my mom had been living at my grandma's (they had been fighting too much), he wanted me to get a computer back from her. I tried to look for it, but Grandma has a storage area downstairs that is locked and so many other areas that it could have been hidden when I visited. He is also mad that I am still talking to my mom. Yet the whole time I lived in his home by myself and did not talk with her, he still spoke with her and I would see them on the phone together all the time.

I said, "If you didn't like her so much, then why are you sending her pictures of a dog and stuff?" And then he hung up. I feel like I am in the middle and I love them both so much. I just want them both to be happy. I think it's a good thing I am going to Italy.

# MARISSA D'ANGELO

# 22
## REVISITING ITALY

*6* Aprile 2017

I just got on the plane to Italy. The first stop is Lisbon, Portugal. This will be an overnight flight. I hope everything goes ok. I actually got kind of lucky because it has been pouring, lightning and thundering all day, but it stopped and turned into a rainbow and sunny skies literally thirty minutes before my departure. Isn't that crazy?!

I changed my seat last night so I would have a window seat, but a mom wanted to be next to her son, so I gave it up. Now I am in the middle aisle seat, which is sucky, but it's ok. The mom was so thankful, and I know if I had a kid, I would want to be next to them, too, on a plane ride. It's ok, no big deal. Well, I'm going to try to get comfortable here. I know I won't sleep much, but maybe I can get just a few hours of sleep.

7 Aprile 2017

Adesso lo sono sull treno andare a Roma di Bologna. (Now I am on the train going to Rome from Bologna) Maria met me at the airport. But for whatever reason, I didn't get a stamp coming into Italy. Hm...I'm trying my best to stay awake...

I was thinking a lot on the plane about how short life is and how many people take it all for granted so easily. People take one another for granted too easily. It is very sad.

Oh...so...tired... I NEED TO STAY AWAKE!

That was a good ten-minute nap...I couldn't fight the urge to sleep. Ten more minutes till we are in Rome, though. I really think I will go right to sleep. My nose hurts because I fell asleep on my book and my hands hurt too, 'cause I fell asleep on them as well.

Io sono in letto adesso! Io voglio dormire. Ma, lo bisogno parlare a tu prima. Oggi era bene! Io sono content essere in Italia. Devo meglio practica con italiano poi è così. Ci sono un carne (barking?) vicino a finestra. Domani, Io dormirò ritardo! Andiamo (mia famiglia con mi) a Minturno vedere tutti in famigilia di Minturno. Io sono molto grazie per tutte loro fanno per mi. Buonanotte. (I am in bed now! I want to sleep. But, I need to talk to you first. Today was great! I am happy to be in Italy. I need more practice with Italian but it's ok. There are dogs barking next to the window. Tomorrow, I will sleep late! We are going to Minturno to see everyone in the family from Minturno. I am very thankful for all they do for me. Goodnight.)

8 Aprile 2017

Io dormito molto bene. Io mangiato Corne Flakes con latte fresco, una mela e cioccolato per colazione. La amica di Maria visitator en la mattina. Io scrivo con il gatto. La doccia era caldo per due minuti poi era freddo piú del tempo. Io penso scrivere in il giornale é bene e fará meglio parlare e scrivere in Italiano. Sta note vedremo la famiglia in Minturno. In dieci minuti andremo a

Fontagna di Trevi.

Io penso non voglio essere con qualsiasi uomo. Io voglio essere con luómo chi é un scrittore, lettore, operaio, cuoco, e mi fa ridere. Lui conosce che cosa fare in problem.

Tutti é bene. Io non voglio vedere un uomo. È cosi. Mario, Maria, e mi – Andiamo Minturno in due ore. La mia famiglia sono in Minturno. Dormiamo in Minturno sta sera e Andiamo Capri domani! Loro parlano in Italiano. É dificile, poi devo practicare. É molto caldo ecco!! Io ho un vestito! Io devo comprare la comicia per la amica, Mike. Lui vuole camicia le Danielli di Rosso – fùtbol. Il gatto, La Mucca, è la mia amica. La mucca = the cow. The cat has spots, so that is why they call her the cow. Otro gatto è molto, perchè I don't know.

(Everything is great. I do not want to see a man. It is ok. Mario, Maria and I—We go to Minturno in two hours. The family is in Minturno. We sleep in Minturno tonight and we go to Capri tomorrow! They speak in Italian. It is difficult, but I need to practice. It is very hot now!! I have a dress! I need to buy a shirt for my friend, Mike. He wants a shirt for Danielli di Rosso for soccer. The cat, La Mucca, is my friend. La mucca means cow. The cat has spots, so that is why they call her the cow. The other cat is mean, because I don't know.)

We walked a lot in Rome today. I am outside writing in you right now and it is very, very hot. Unbelievably hot. I went to Minturno to see the family, and it was great. However, I realized how bad I am at understanding spoken Italian. It is hard to listen as they go so fast. I need to learn more vocabulary and just be around it more often.

9 Aprile 2017

Io sono la nuova amica! Il nome di lei é Mina. È buffo perché uno Mina (il cane dell amia papa) uscita mia vita e adesso il nuova Mina entra la mia vita. Penso Mina è bene. Voglio parlare con Mina piú. Lei parla in Inglese e Io parlo in Italiano. Parliamo con Whatsapp. Io sono contento avere una amica in Italia! É dificile avere una amica in Uniti Stadi...Spero che possiamo essere amiche. Io ho andato a Capri! Noi usiamo il treno andare a Napoli. Segundo, noi usciamo ferry (Non lo so come se dice) andare Capri. Io vedo dormire pronto. Io sono rosso da il sole. Il tempo per dormire! Buonanotte!

(I have a new friend! Her name is Mina. Is funny because 1 Mina—my dad's dog was named Mina—and now the new Mina has entered my life. I think Mina is great. I want to talk with Mina more. She speaks in English and I speak in Italian. We talk with WhatsApp. I am happy to have a friend in Italy! It is difficult to have a friend in the United States...I hope that we can be friends. I have to go to Capri! We are using the train to go to Naples. Second, we are using the ferry (I don't know how to say) to go to Capri. I am ready to sleep. I am red from the sun. It is time for bed! Goodnight!)

10 Aprile 2017

Andiamo a Roma da Minturno adesso. Quando ho dormito, Io ho sognato chi eros u una nave. Un giorno, saliró le montagne di Italia.

The fact that these same mountains were in view when my Nonna Maria and Nonno Alessandro fell in love is crazy. I think if I meet the right guy, I will not feel held back. I have this cool fantasy in my head where I am greeting an Italian boy and we kiss one another on the cheeks in greeting, but then all of a sudden he brings me in for a kiss. Just a cool fantasy that won't happen, but nice to dream.

The cat that is next to me, not Mucca but the mean one, looks so mad at me. I feel she may slap me any second. Mario just said I can take a walk if I want and I think I may.

It was a nice walk. I only got lost three times! I saw a school, which was cool. The time I got lost, I actually used a map on my phone. I eventually was able to get back in one piece here though. Giulio called on the phone. This is Maria's son, so he is my 3$^{rd}$ cousin or so. I was confused who it was at first. I think Mario and I are going to go on the bus to go to the center of Rome. I need to change my socks from walking so much. Mina is coming to the United States maybe someday! She wants me to show her everything and I am so excited because that means I'll get to see a lot, too! At some point, I need to warn her about the crazies, though, but I'm sure she knows that. There are crazy people everywhere. This is really cool that I made a new friend!

I took the train with Mario to go to the center of Rome. We saw a lot. We went to an Old Jewish town and got baccili, which means cod fish. It was really good. I still haven't been able to find a shirt for Mike. He said he'd give me money for it. It's for a soccer player.

Mina said she would come with me to Verona because I said I might want to go there. However, it takes hours upon hours to get there. And I do not want to be away from my family in Rome for that long because I feel like that's rude. But maybe we can just meet up in Rome.

Anyway, today Mario also brought me to a church that was basically made of three churches. They were destroyed, so now the middle part of the church was reused and built over for one big church. I wouldn't have known that if I was only passing by, so I found it very interesting. We also walked over to this ship that is permanently docked in the middle of the center of Rome and it is a hospital!

I got back and lay down from going on the long walk with Mario. It was really nice! I am glad that I went; he is very knowledgeable of everything in Rome. I am not alone, but feel lonely. If that makes sense at all? Giulio came over to my room and asked if I wanted to look out the telescope. I used a Russian spy's telescope to see the moon, and it was so amazing! I enjoyed sitting at their table and watching Giulio play some games when everyone else had gone to bed. He's working on something with his 3D printer. I feel very welcomed. When I feel that way, I don't usually go back to my bedroom, but stay out in the main area. I am reading a book and really enjoyed the quote that I found from it:

"None of us are getting out of here alive, so please stop treating yourself like an afterthought. Eat delicious food. Walk in the sunshine. Jump in the ocean. Say the truth that you're carrying in your heart like hidden treasure. Be silly. Be kind. Be weird. There's no time for anything else." —Christopher Walken

11 Aprile 2017

I went to the center of Rome alone by using the subway!

I felt so great about myself. I actually went inside the coliseum and went to the Roman Forum again. I cut the line to go into the coliseum (shhhh) because it was just me and I pretended to be with another family. I got the blue soccer sweatshirt for Mike and some fried meatballs, too. Oh, and of course I got some gelato to snack on. I met a group of Americans, and they were nice. When I came back to my relative's place, I passed out completely! I think I slept for like two hours for my nap! I was so tired. On the subway back, there was a cute man. But I missed my chance so I'm just repeatedly telling myself that he was gay, maybe. That way, I don't get sad about missing the opportunity. Tomorrow, Maria and I will go to Assisi. This was a place I always wanted to go because my Nonni Maria gave me a book about St. Francis of Assisi when I was just a child. I made banana cream pie for them, but had to change some parts since I couldn't find everything in the Italian supermarkets. They didn't have Cool Whip, so I used whipped cream instead, which made it end up being like a soup. The cat fell asleep on the bed that I sleep on, so I'm going to leave the door open while I sleep so it can escape.

I can't stop thinking of how badly I wish to be held and kissed. I don't know why, but I am longing for some kind of human connection like that. I think it is better off I don't meet someone here in Italy, obviously, because I have to go back at some point. Goodnight!

12 Aprile 2017

I had many dreams last night. One that I specifically remember was that I was getting a quick bite (maybe...well, probably one of those amazing fried rice balls) and I sat at the table. An Italian man was looking at me. We ended up sharing our life stories and were there for a long time. He was in the military and ah...I forget what else. But it was pretty cool.

I remember when I got on the train to go back from the coliseum, this guy with the bluest eyes made my heart stop. I was just thinking about it. And maybe, in my past life, I was with someone with very light blue eyes because they seem to have a way of making my heart stop.

Today, I ended up going to Assisi and my, what a beautiful place! It tops all the places I have been to thus far. It is on a hill and overlooked pretty much everything in Assisi. There was one church I went to that had a church within it, which used to be the church where St. Francis prayed. It was so small and simple. I liked it a lot. Part of the ceiling of the smaller church displayed the night sky with small stars and such. It was very nice. I would like to attend a small church like that. I want to be with a guy, but maybe it is just not meant to be. Maybe I'm just meant to be alone. Here, I see so many couples together. Hand in hand, lip on lip, laughing together (rare, but still) and taking care of one another. I want that. But I think it is not meant for me.

13 Aprile 2017

I am on my way back to America. I had a great time in Italy. I learned a lot about history, my family and also myself. I learned I am capable of so much on my own. I learned I don't actually need a man, but I would like one. I would like that very much. But I guess maybe God saved me the trouble by not finding love in Italy. I wouldn't be able to be with him. My favorite place I visited was Italy. It was so peaceful and tranquil. I could picture St. Francis walking to and from the small church that he prayed at all while living a very humble lifestyle.

Goodnight!

If someone wants to be with you, they won't make any excuses. They won't back away and be a coward. They will fight for you and want to be with you.

# 23

## ONE MORE TIME

Just when I was ready to completely shut myself out from dating, I decided to scroll through Tinder a final time. My previous experiences with it were ok, but I didn't really click with anyone and of course there were several sketchy people that if I looked them up on Facebook, it had shown they were in a relationship. It was difficult to find people that were genuine.

There was one interesting picture of a guy named George. He was holding a hawk and its wings were almost spread out fully. I swiped right. He seemed interesting enough. After just a few moments, a message popped up.

*George: Hey, how are you?*

This was a new one. Usually I'd get a "sup" or "heyyyy." I answered, and we ended up talking back and forth and finally exchanged snapchat usernames. I did this in case he turned out to be a weirdo, so he wouldn't have my number. He turned out to be very interesting and our conversations actually held substance, which was hard to find. We planned to meet, and I chose the place that we would go for dinner.

On my way there, I was on the phone with my mom.

"So, you're going on a date?"

"Yeah, well—it's just like a casual date to meet one another." I wasn't getting my hopes up.

"Ok. Well, be safe and don't go anywhere alone with him." She always said this as if I was stupid, but I knew she was just worried about me.

I was still on the phone with her when I pulled into the restaurant's parking lot. Something wasn't right because the sign for "Orzo" was removed and there were no cars in the parking lot when there should've been since it was suppertime. No one was there.

"I think the restaurant closed down, Mom. Oh no, he probably thinks this is a set-up!"

I turned my car around in the parking lot but decided to park so I could figure everything out.

"Ok, I'll let you go. Have fun and be careful." We hung up.

I opened up Snapchat and saw some missed messages from him.

*George: Hey, I think I'm lost. I'm at Puerto Vallerta.*

This was a restaurant right next to the parking lot where I parked.

*Marissa: Ok, meet me in front of Puerto Vallerta.*

I got my bag and walked over to that restaurant. A man with a red shirt that said "Chick's" on the right side of the chest walked toward me. When I got closer, I noticed his light blue eyes and fair skin. His hair was short. He had told me he just got a haircut recently. He looked good! Now here's to hoping he wasn't just another man looking to get laid.

"Hey! The place that we were supposed to go to was right there." I pointed behind Puerto Vallerta. "I had no idea it was closed!"

"Oh, so you weren't standing me up then?" he joked.

I laughed. "Wanna go to Wood 'n' Tap?" He agreed, and we headed over. It was like two minutes away from where we were. I'm still not sure why we didn't go to Puerto Vallerta. When we got to the restaurant and the host asked how many, I answered two. The host sat us down and said someone would be right with us. I opened up the menu, but we continued talking about how he thought I had stood him up and he was about to leave.

"What're you gonna get?" I asked, hoping it might influence my decision, too.

"I'll get a burger," he said without hesitation.

"Oh, that sounds good!" I said. I ran my eyes down the menu. Appetizers...I'd want fried calamari...sandwiches...ribs...

"What about you?" he asked.

"I wanna get the ribs, but they're too messy."

"Get them! I don't care," he smiled.

When the waiter came, we made our order, and I went with the ribs.

"So, I'm glad you didn't make me drive all this way and ditch me." He smiled.

"Oh, I wouldn't have! The place I wanted to go to changed ownership so many times. I had no idea," I replied. I felt bad. He must've been so confused. I know I would've been if I were invited to a place that didn't exist.

"It's ok! So, what do you do?" he asked.

"I'm a teacher. Well, right now I am a substitute, but next year I'll be a teacher's assistant." I was currently getting my master's degree in Special Education. It was also pretty difficult to find a job. Everyone wanted you to have years and years of experience as a teacher to become a teacher. Catch-22.

"Oh, that's really cool."

"How about you?" I was very interested. Was it something to do with birds? He had a hawk in his hands.

"I just graduated a little while ago from the Merchant Marine. Was away at sea. I'm looking for a tow boat business to buy," he said.

"Ah, that's so cool!" I said back. "So you've been all around the world then, huh?"

"Yeah, Africa, Singapore, so many places. I'd have to say the coolest place I went to was Singapore."

When the food was served, I did find myself making a mess of my face and fingers. We both laughed. It felt nice talking to him. I told him about my travel dreams and he talked more about the places he visited while in college. We made plans to play some Nintendo 64 later. I was a bit old school and knew most people loved it too. Mario Kart & Super Smash Bros. were the main two games I played on the Nintendo 64.

Months went by and I found myself spending almost every day with him after that. So much so that I snuck one of my keys to my apartment in his pocket. He ended up moving in. It only made sense since we spent so much time together.

When I put together things for teaching, he would help me. There was one time when I was an assistant for a classroom that I brought my work home with me and I had to make little books for each student that were leveled per request from the teacher. This was chaos because I didn't know the shortcut of how to do it at first and was putting each individual page together. He was the stapler. Gradually, as we got more used to one another and comfortable, I realized we were actually very different. But I loved spending time with him.

# 24
## ARE YOU STILL THERE?

One of the biggest things about living in Connecticut was being able to take a train into New York City. I woke up that morning and was so excited to go out into the city before heading to the Broadway show I grew up seeing each year, The Rockettes. It was quite difficult to wake *George* up, though.

"Come on, wake up. It's ten o'clock, we can go now!" I said, hyper and impatient to go. I already made breakfast, took care of the cats, and all that was left to do was to leave.

He groaned and rolled over. Aggravating. I walked away and decided to give it more time and came back about an hour or so later after watching some cartoons.

"Hey," I whispered. "We're gonna have a great day together. Let's go so we can enjoy it."

"No, you just go." His words struck me, and I felt like I was slapped in the face.

I decided to push on. "We had this all planned out, this special day. Please, let's just go, ok?"

"If you don't want to wait, then we're not going," he said and rolled over. I walked out of the room in tears and felt my legs fold from underneath me as I fell back into the couch in the other room. I was so upset. This was going to be so special. and it was already eleven o'clock. I was so used to going earlier because spending the money to buy a ticket into New York was more worth it if you spent more time there. Why spend the money only for a few hours?

After a while longer and more arguing, he finally came out and decided to get on the road with me toward the train station. I was really biting my lip, but still wanted to go to New York, so I pushed my anger to the side. By the time we got everything together, we left around eleven-thirty or so and didn't speak much on the train ride. I looked out the window at the different people as we would stop at each station. Some of them were families and others were just single women or men that carried a briefcase and were likely going to work.

I turned and saw that *George* was sleeping. I turned my music up on my headphones and rested my head back, too. After just a few songs, I looked at my phone and scrolled through the Snapchat stories. There was a random story that would stop on an emoji that predicted your future. I chose to give it a shot, even though I didn't believe in it much. It landed on a sad emoji with bandages around its head. I closed the phone. It could've been something nice, like a happy emoji or even one with its tongue out, since I was planning to get some delicious food in New York. But no, a wounded emoji. I took this as metaphorical for how I felt inside and locked the phone, resting my head back again.

When we finally got to Grand Central Station, we stayed close by to one another and walked into the huge lobby. I stared up at the ceiling as I always would whenever I got to Grand Central. The Constellations that were painted on the ceiling were always so interesting to look at.

"Ok, we're here. Where are we headed?" he asked.

"Let's go to the main area, like in Times Square," I said. I was a little hungry and was certain that we'd find some food there. We didn't have enough time to stop at The Hershey Store or M&M Store, which were frequents, but that was OK. We headed over toward Olive Garden because a lot of other restaurants were there. The line was out the door. We kept walking past and ended up at Junior's. I looked at their menu and saw they had some really yummy cheesecakes. This was the one! It had a long wait, but we eventually got in. We had to make our Broadway show, but had time to stop for a little bit. I forget exactly what I got, but they had a lot of classic food there and it gave me a 50s vibe that I loved.

"So, what do you think you're going to get for dessert?" I asked.

"I don't know," he said, looking down at his food and continuing to eat.

"How is your coaching going on the weekends?" I asked, trying to make conversation.

"Good," he said. I was trying here, but not sure what the sour mood was from. We made it past the morning, and we were here, so we should be enjoying it.

"What's wrong?" I asked and then continued eating.

"I'm trying to eat. Do I need to be interrogated?" he asked. It was silence after that. Another slap in my face. Was I too sensitive? I gulped down my food hard, even though I wasn't hungry any longer.

When we were walking toward Broadway, he apologized and said he was just trying to eat.

"It's ok. Let's just go and enjoy the show," I said. "I'm going to call my mom really quick before we go in to make sure everything is ok."

It rang several times, but she finally picked up on almost the last ring.

"Hello?" she said. I could hear how tired she was.

"Hey, I am in New York City now and we're about to go into the show," I said.

"Ok, I'm over Grandma's. Have fun," she replied slowly between each word. It wasn't slurred speech though, not quite. Something was off, though.

"Are you ok?" I asked.

"Yes, just a little tired. I'll go lie down on Grandma's couch before I go home," she said.

"That's a good idea. I'll call you after, love you." I said.

"Love you too. Bye," she responded.

*George* could tell something was up. "Everything ok? Let's just enjoy the day, ok?" He gave me a hug, and we walked into the theater. The red carpets and extravagant décor really set the scene. As soon as you stepped foot inside, you KNEW you were in Broadway. We got a hot cocoa that came in a souvenir cup and some snacks. We were just a bit early and ate our snacks while we waited.

I turned to *George*. "Thank you for coming. I really appreciate it. I know this isn't your thing, but thank you for coming."

He gave me a kiss on my cheek, "Sure thing, I love you."

I smiled, and all felt well again. We watched the show, and it was the same amazing show as always. I don't even really know my favorite part. Oh actually…yes, yes I do. There's one part where all the Rockettes come out in lines as wooden soldiers, and they have very stiff movements, as if they don't bend their legs and they march in their order. They formed different patterns, too. Instead of a straight line, they would have several, and it would almost look like an asterisk if you were looking down from above them. From this placement, they would walk forward, and the asterisk looked like it was spinning. At the very end, they stood in a very still line with everyone and a cannon was shot from one side. From the very front of the line, the soldiers slowly—very, very slowly—fell back onto one another so perfectly. Describing it doesn't do it any justice, but it's got to be my favorite part of the show. I was so happy after this and called my mom to tell her how it went. She didn't answer, so I focused on getting to the train with *George*. The train was almost packed, but we managed to find two seats next to one another that we could sit in.

I tried to call her again and then, with no answer, just laid my head back and decided to try to sleep. No luck, as usual. When I got bored, I would scroll through the news on my phone and when we got out of the tunnels with no service, I opened up safari and clicked on the news tab that I had saved. It refreshed from the page that it was on earlier. At the very top of the stories was a picture. A picture that would forever change my life.

There was a tanker truck on its side, and to its left was another car. It was a silver Lexus but wasn't just any silver Lexus…because it had a circular magnet on its side and a German Shephard picture was on that magnet. The front of the car was smashed in. No room for a driver even. It was my mom's car.

I started hyperventilating. "George, George." I couldn't speak. I just handed him the phone.

"Oh, come on, it's just a silver Lexus. Many people have those." He tried to see the good. But there was no good. I brought my shaky hand over to the phone and pointed to the magnet.

"She has that magnet exactly in that place. It's her. It's my mom!" I said, grabbing my phone back. I didn't even take the time to read the news story. Instead, I called every hospital I could think of. It was closest to Yale New Haven Hospital, so I tried there first.

"Hel-Hello, my mom is there, I think," I said, my whole body shaking, my voice trembling. I gave her name.

"Ok sweetie, let me transfer you to triage," I heard a click and someone else came on the phone.

"Hi, my mom is there." I gave the first and last name and spelled it out for them, barely able to think straight.

"We don't have anyone by that name, honey. Sorry," she said. We hung up. I tried my dad, and he didn't answer. I tried my grandma, which was the last resort, but I had to. I didn't want to upset her but had no choice because I needed to know what was going on and maybe she knew.

"Hello? Marissa?" Grandma picked up the phone.

"Grandma, do you know where my mom is?" I asked.

"A doctor called here; she's going into surgery now. She was in a bad accident," she said.

"So, she's still alive?? She's still there??" I asked, frantic.

"As far as I know, Marissa."

"I'm on a train now and I'll be back soon and I'm coming right there then we'll go to the hospital, ok?" I said, and we hung up shortly after.

At this point, the part of the train that we were on had heard how frantic I was and many people surrounded me and were giving me their prayers and kind words. They felt very bad. The rest of the train ride was the longest ride I ever had coming back from New York. I didn't know what to think. Could she speak? Could she eat? Did she lose any limbs? Was she going to survive? Was I going to be without my mom already?

I called my dad again, and he told me all about the accident and exaggerated a little bit, saying they needed a helicopter to take her out of there. We decided to go with him originally, but then he got very mad that George was going to come. I assured him there was no way I could drive in this state, but he still wanted it to just be me and him. I told him I would bring him later on, but he refused. His way or the highway. We hung up with no plans to meet up. Sometimes, it was like this.

When we got back home, George drove my grandma and me because I was too much of a shaken mess to be trusted to drive anywhere and we headed to the hospital. We went right to the ER.

"Hi, my mom is here," I said, again giving her name.

"Oh, we don't have her." I was going to flip out. My heart was racing more than it had been already.

Another nurse came by and overheard our conversation. "Oh, maybe she's the Jane Doe?" I gave them the accident location and everything and they allowed me back. When the other nurse had referred to my mother as a Jane Doe, I didn't know what to expect. I was a big fan of Grey's Anatomy and just remembered the Jane Doe's being unrecognizable and all bandaged up. I pictured the worst.

The nurse led us back and then we went up to a surgical room where we waited for hours watching the screen, waiting for my mom's surgery to change to "In Recovery" so we could see her. At some point, a surgeon came over and explained to us there was so much shrapnel in her leg that they were making sure to get it out so an infection didn't start. They left, and it was a few hours before the screen finally changed. A doctor brought us back to her, and she had her leg wrapped up in a huge cast and one arm was in another cast. She also had a neck brace on.

"Mom, can you hear me? Are you still there?" I asked.

"Marissa," she mumbled and cried. As soon as she had woken up and the medication was wearing off a bit, she screamed out in pain and cried and cried. A nurse came in and put more medication in through her IV.

"It'll be ok, Mom. You're going to be ok," I said and touched her hand. We waited there for a while, but she was hanging on. I had no idea, nor did anyone have an idea of what would be in store after this or what condition she would eventually be in if she got better, but she made it to the hospital. That was step one.

# MARISSA D'ANGELO

# 25
## WHAT TO DO?

March 10, 2018

So much is going on in my life right now. It will be so hard to tell you everything. Yesterday, I was on my way home from Target and I thought to stop over my parents' house. I wasn't going to, but I did. As soon as I opened the back door, my mom came running over to me and clung herself to me and said, "Thank God you're here. I need to get out of here. Your dad has been so pissed at me and I don't know what is going on with him."

She refused to go near my dad and Dad just denied whatever happened and said she was crazy. That's the typical thing that would happen. Mom was really frightened. I ended up just bringing her to my grandma's house, which was the routine. I don't know how to process any of this. Ever since their accident, they have been different people and I never know which way is up or down with them. I just want all the drama with my parents to stop. I want them to be happy. That's all. It breaks my heart.

March 11, 2018

Last night, I went to bring my mom some clothes and things over to my grandma's 'cause that's where she was still staying. While I was getting the clothes from my dad's, my mom had called him, and he put it on speakerphone and she was asking to move back. And I was so disgusted because here I was, in the middle, going back and forth. I worked seven days a week, any extra time I had was spent going back and forth. I went on my way to grandma's anyway and when I arrived, there was an ambulance right in front of her place. My mom went out to smoke and talk to my dad on the phone and had tripped and fallen straight onto her back. So the ambulance was taking her away as soon as I pulled up. I saw her inside the ambulance and she kept having muscle spasms and really didn't look right. She kept jerking to the left and the right. Almost as if she was having a seizure.

I called George crying, and was barely able to get a word out. Eventually I did, and we met at the hospital. I begged her to just stay at grandma's because I knew my parents were codependent and shared the medication. "Marissa, just forget about me and move to Florida," she said. After a while of pleading with her, I had to leave. The next morning, I called the hospital that she was at and they said she had been discharged. My dad got a taxi for her to go to his place. Dad purposely "butt dialed" me so I could hear what she was saying. She said she knows she has been lying to me and then she told my dad to check his phone to see if he was butt dialing someone, and then he hung up. He called me a minute later and I said I heard her and he said I was going crazy, that it didn't happen. Maybe I am going crazy. I want everyone to be okay.

March 12, 2018

Mom was discharged and signed herself out of the hospital at 9:30 a.m. yesterday. My dad had kept saying she wasn't there. I had to threaten to call the police and file a missing person's report for them to finally tell me where she was. I literally went there and she tried to hide from me. When I finally talked to her, she said there was no hope or anything anyone could do to change things. I was so upset. She was saying she should've died in the car accident she was in back in December. I guess she doesn't know how I felt to have almost lost her. I feel abandoned. I feel broken. George is telling me to forget about them, but that is not easy to do. They are my parents and I love them with all my heart. I feel like I did lose my mom.

March 18, 2018

I look at myself in the mirror and I can see how stressed I am. I can see how much all the stress is taking it out on me physically, emotionally, and mentally. I want to move on from it. I am tired of being upset by all of this.

I am looking at jobs in Connecticut and Florida. George may be moving to Florida. I'm not sure yet what is happening with his job, so that's why I am applying to both states. We had his friend, Brandon, and his girlfriend over for corned beef and cabbage. It was really good and simple, too. I had just put it into the slow cooker and it cooked itself. He helped me prepare for them coming over by vacuuming and mopping. He was super helpful.

All that I have gone through has been damaging. At

random moments, I feel like breaking down and crying. I just want to go home and lay down in the dark under my blankets. It is hard to pull myself out of this depression.

March 24, 2018

It is really early in the morning, but my heart feels like it is going to beat out of its chest. I just do not feel at ease at all. I really love my parents and them doing this to themselves is just awful. It makes me so upset. I never know when I am going to get a call that one of them is gone.

Why did medication have to take over their lives? It's not fair. I don't know what I did to deserve this. I can't even fall asleep.

March 25, 2018

I have been coping a little bit better. The past few days were very hard. Each day, my heart felt as though it was racing. Even in a completely quiet room, I had flashbacks to the screaming and yelling and sirens flashing. George and I are on our way to visit Florida. I do not want to run away. But I want to be happy. I have tried to help my parents and no matter what, they still get themselves back to square one over and over again. I guess it has to come from them. I am looking outside the window right now from the plane. It's over the ocean and we are just going onto land. I can see the outline of the coast and it is beautiful.

We ended up staying in Florida for just a few nights. George got very sick, but we managed to go to the beach once and there was a hot tub at the place, so that was nice. I felt really bad that he was sick, though. It's ok though, he's better now!

May 6, 2018

I've been having very bad nightmares of flashbacks. And every time I go there now, they are both fighting nonstop. I offer to bring Mom to Grandma's so they can have space from one another and she just refuses every time. I was trying to bring her another phone too because somehow her phones keep breaking. The one I had just gotten her was really smashed and broken. When I walked downstairs, my dad had been using a knife on his arm because he supposedly got burned, so he was trying to rip the top layer off. I just can't take it anymore. There's only so much I can take. I don't know what to do. I can't win. I feel like crying and I just feel no motivation, although I keep going somehow. It is just so depressing. I want them to be happy.

May 8, 2018

I need to remember I am strong. I need to remember it will be ok. My world feels like it is falling apart, but I just need to keep going.

# 26
## STAY?

May 24, 2018
I went to Maryland for a short time with George. He is looking into getting a job here and everything seems to be falling into place to move here instead of Florida. My dad found out about my possible move with George and he is very against it. He thinks that he is trying to isolate me from everyone, but I feel like it could also be good to get away from everyone since I've been continuously in the middle all the time. When we went, I tried to get some job interviews there, too. I spoke with my mom and she sounded very sad and deflated. No energy, really. I heard them both arguing. I got up and headed over to pick her up and bring her to my grandma's because I didn't want an altercation to happen between them. I was too late. The police were called. This is more of a reason why I feel like I should just get out of the state.

May 31, 2018
This is a sad time. I think my parents almost took too much of their medication last week. It is out of my hands. Now, I can't wait to move. I feel so guilty for leaving. I feel like my

moving is causing all of this, but I have to keep reminding myself that is not true because even while I lived in Connecticut, there have been so many issues. I woke up feeling sad about my family. Very sad. We are set to move July 1$^{st}$ of this year and I know my parents are going to feel destroyed inside. I feel like I have been left with no choice, though.

# 27

# WHOOPS...

There were so many jobs that I applied for. One place called me back, and the job was for a part-time special education teacher and part time Italian teacher. George and I left very early one morning so I could make the interview, so I was completely exhausted, to say the least. When I came into that interview, I didn't have to wait one moment and the principal had already come out along with her assistant and the global studies committee of some sort, since I would be teaching a language. The principal looked fairly young and had blonde hair about shoulder length. She wore a darker dress suit and was very friendly and welcoming.

"Hello Marissa, thanks for coming in!" she exclaimed. "Come right with me." I smiled and thanked her, then followed down the hall and into the back room where the global studies people and assistant principal waited at a long table.

As soon as I sat down with my résumé before me, they each introduced who they were.

"As part of your job, you will be teaching Italian. We wanted to do a quick run through of the language component, but mostly you will be teaching the culture and traditions of Italy."

"Oh, that sounds great! I studied abroad over there and have family there too, so I go back to stay with them." The lady already began taking notes.

"Tell me about where you went!" she said, seemingly interested.

"Well, I went all over. Lived in Rome and walked everywhere to visit the churches. I went to the gladiators pagan worshipping sites, ancient Rome, the coliseum. But I also visited Florence, Venice, Ravenna, Bologna, Capri, Naples, Pompeii, Assisi, Ariccia and Minturno."

"Wow, that's a lot of places! Which one would you say was your favorite?" the principal chimed in. It was very easy to talk about Italy. The words flowed out like water.

"Pompeii and Assisi were my favorites. Pompeii was a huge piece of history—a town—preserved in place in a way. Many people were encased in lava and ash. It shows their last moments, and it's amazing that it is still intact to this day." I stopped, realizing I was talking too much. They all looked at one another, then one of the global studies teachers spoke.

"And Assisi?" I knew I should've just finished.

"I went to Assisi because I always looked up to St. Francis of Assisi from the moment my Nonni gave me a book about him. My cousin brought me there, and it wasn't crowded at all. Just pure calm. The church that St. Francis worshipped in is still intact and they actually built a larger church over it to better protect it. It's amazing. Just outside, you'll be able to look over everything and see mountains in the distance." I smiled back at the memory.

"That's amazing! It sounds like you'd have a lot to share with the kids! Alright, let's have a short conversation in Italian. Introduce yourself and tell what you like." That seemed easy enough. She was still writing, and I felt shaky from all the tea I drank to stay awake.

"Mi nombre es Marissa Mi piace l'aragosta e dolce. Come sta?" They did not reply back to me, but thanked me and said they would call me. The next thing I knew it, I was in George's car heading out and a realization enveloped me.

"Shoot!!" I yelled randomly as he drove away.

"What?" he asked.

"I introduced myself in Spanish instead of Italian." I did not receive a call back, to say the least.

# 28

# A FRESH START

I truly never got a call back. A few weeks went by, and I was scared out of my mind that I hadn't been hired yet. I did get another interview as an ACC teacher. I knew this was Special Education, but wasn't quite sure what ACC entailed or even what it stood for. The job would provide me with a purpose in life. This time I drove there and made sure to get enough sleep the night before.

At the very front of the building, there was a triangular roof with a circle shaped window in the brick. When I walked up toward the entrance, there was a square with two footprints in front of the door and next to that, on the wall, a scanner and button. I pressed it. The door buzzed open, and I walked into the main office and saw three secretary desks. I turned to the desk that was closest to the window.

"Hey, I'm Marissa. I've got an interview for the ACC teacher position," I said to the lady behind the desk. She had short blonde hair with a bunch of highlights.

"Ok, have a seat right there!" she said as she gestured over to the seats that were next to me. I sat down and held my résumé binder close to my chest.

"How are you today?"

"Oh, I'm good. Hoping to go to the beach after this. Yesterday, I typed beach into my GPS and ended up on private property. Gonna keep exploring later. Do you know of any good beaches for the public?" I figured I'd ask.

"Oh yeah! Sandy Point, and there's a lot on the Eastern Shore, too." I nodded my head and pretended to understand those references. Just then, the principal came out of her office.

"Hey there, come on back!" She smiled and waved then headed back into her office. She had a Southern accent and blonde hair with rosy cheeks. Her presence was immediately welcoming. In her office, there was a desk immediately in the corner, but a circular table on the other side. We went over to sit at the table.

At first, we talked about my previous work experiences and then what brought me to Maryland. I also found out that ACC stood for Alternate Curriculum Classroom. I would have just a few students in the classroom where I would teach them an alternate curriculum. This reminded me a bit of a self-contained classroom where students with special needs received the majority of their subject-area instruction in an alternate classroom. The students would still attend Morning Meeting, Cultural Arts, Lunch and Recess with their general education peers. Then, she asked a question that I was never asked at an interview before.

"What was one of your most challenging moments either in school or personal life?" One specific thing came to mind. I was hesitant about sharing at first but knew it would surely be coming straight from my heart.

"My mom was in a head on collision with an oil tanker truck last year. I found out by seeing her car on the news." At this point, her jaw dropped, and she was not writing any notes about anything, just giving me her full attention. I continued. "She was ok, but had a long road after that toward recovery. She wasn't able to feed herself or even walk, hold things or write. Many things we can do we take for granted. This was challenging because so much was out of my hands and all I could do was support her emotionally. That's it." I felt a tear stream down my cheek and it touched my lips, leaving a salty taste in my mouth. My face suddenly grew warm and my palms sweaty. I took a deep breath and quickly wiped the tear so as not to let her know or make it more awkward. Maybe I shouldn't have brought it up.

"Honey, what an enormous challenge that must have been. It truly reflects on the strong person you are today. Thank you for sharing that story with me. It helped shape the person you are today."

"Thank you." I smiled. She smiled back, and we left on a good note. I was feeling much better about leaving this interview. So good that when I headed out, I saw another woman waiting where I had sat and said, "Good luck!" and turned to the secretaries, "Have a great summer!"

"Hope you find your beach!"

MARISSA D'ANGELO

# 29
## PLEASE DON'T GO

Although I moved out of state, I would talk to my parents every day. I did miss them a lot, but I felt like I needed to leave and put distance between us so I could go on with my life and not get sucked into the problems they would have. I never wanted to take sides nor had I ever tried, but whenever there were issues such as my mom taking medication or vice versa, I would just try to separate them by bringing my mother over to my grandma's house. Someway, somehow, she would always end up back over my dad's and no matter what I did, it didn't seem like anything truly helped. I would even come there on my lunches from work and if they would call me, I'd come right away without question so I could separate them before things got worse.

The previous year that I had visited for Christmas, they were out of it on and off; so, I was a bit skeptical about this visit, but all my life they were my Christmas. In the beginning, everything was so nice but unfortunately because of the addiction there was no knowing what would happen. I spent a few days at George's family's house and then went over to my family's. I remember as soon as I drove up, my dad was already outside and had his arms out, ready to hug me. He was very muscular. His hugs were the greatest feeling in the world. I got out of my car and he came up to me and hugged me. I felt my feet leave the ground as he picked me up in the air.

"I missed you, Slim," he said.

"I missed you too, Dad. I'm so glad I could come back home for Christmas," I said, stifling back the tears.

He put me down after a while. I could tell he didn't want to let go.

"I've got the pup in the car, Dad, hang on," I said as I walked around back and got Meadow out. She was a red merle Toy Australian Shephard that weighed about eight or nine pounds. She was basically one giant ball of spunk that I had NO intention of showing to Harley, especially being that was Harley's home and she would look at Meadow as an intruder. As soon as I brought her out of the car, she ran for my dad and started jumping on him like crazy with her butt wagging back and forth.

He bent down and accepted the dozens and dozens of kisses from her. "Hey there, Piglet! What're you doing?!" After a while of kisses, we began to walk down the front sidewalk. He started telling me about the Christmas gifts he just couldn't wait for.

"If I tell you one of the things you're going to get, will you forget?" he said. Of course I wouldn't forget, though! And he knew that. But he just couldn't keep a secret and wanted to tell me so bad.

"Wait till Christmas! I got you so many great things, too!" I said back to him. I could tell he was still going to bring out some gifts, though. We finally got in the door and I ran Meadow upstairs right away to put her in my bedroom with the door closed. I could already hear Harley barking like crazy.

When I walked back downstairs, Harley came running up to me and sniffed me like crazy. My dad walked over to her and said what he would always say to rile her up,

"What did you do? What did you do?" he said as he rubbed her on the side. She was a German Shephard and whined so loud. It felt nice being back home. Everything seemed to be just about the same as when I was growing up. Mom walked over and gave me a hug. She seemed very happy to see me, too. And wow, there was no arguing!

My dad paid his father each month to live at the house I had grown up in. The hope was that he would put it in his name, but he never had any desire to. There was a lot of work that he put into it at the very beginning. In the front, a gray cobblestone walkway went from the driveway to the front porch that was made up of much larger gray cobblestone pieces. Along the walkway, there was a ledge from the garden that was a foot or so up. Behind the garden, there was a large window that looked right into the family room where my family would watch TV and play games on the sofa. Dad had the window blocked out from the other side by putting up a bunch of blankets and things so light wouldn't be let in. I'm not sure what happened to the blinds that had been there. As you walked into the house, the front door was something you wouldn't forget because in order to ring the doorbell, you would have to put your hand inside of a lion statue's mouth and the button was inside. This matched the two larger lion statues out front, on each side of the driveway. Inside was the main foyer and immediately on your right was the living room, which was a smaller version of the TV room. This was honestly a sunroom because the large window on this side let in a lot of sun and my dad didn't ever cover this one up, as he wasn't there too often. If you kept going straight through the foyer, you would find yourself in the kitchen area where the table was and over to the right there was the actual kitchen with a stove, fridge, etc. When I was younger, the kitchen area for the table was a separate section from the actual kitchen you'd cook in. Since then, the wall had been taken out so an open kitchen concept could be created. Past the kitchen was the dining room where we used to use when guests would come over. The dining room set was beautiful. It was dark wood and there was a china cabinet full of glassware. My dad loaded the china cabinet up with different art pieces I painted for him and other things that we had bought at Disney World and the Looney Tunes store. There was one smaller cabinet to the right of the china cabinet, but it did not really have anything on top. The dining room table had broken, and my dad used some type of glue and stacked up tiles to hold it up since one leg broke off. My last memory at this table was when I played Shepherd-opoly the past Christmas with my parents. If you walked back into the kitchen area and kept going, there was the TV room I had mentioned earlier. This used to be the garage, but an addition was built in the early 2000s to add a garage next to that room and insulate the old garage better so it could be used as a family room instead.

Going back the way we had come all the way to the front door, we could then use the stairs to head up. This was a five-bedroom colonial. So when you got up the stairs and to your left there was the master bedroom and beside that was my bedroom. My parents' room also had dark wood furniture with a light tan rug. They had a bathroom in this room that had very nice tile in it going up the sides about halfway up. The tile was a deep, marble blue but was changed over to white marble. When I was very young, I was given the choice of what carpet I wanted and I chose purple. My mom protested against it again and again, but we ended up with purple and that's what we stayed with. Originally, it was Disney Princess themed, and my mom actually sponge painted the entire room, but then it just became a purple and white flower theme at some point. I had white wooden furniture that comprised a bed frame, armoire that sat beside the bed, a mirror dresser that stood directly across from the bed, and a desk on the wall closest to the door. It was nice because the white wood had delicate leaves outlined into it in various places. I remember when my parents were downstairs, and I was supposed to be sleeping, they would ALWAYS hear me even if I was tiptoeing out because the floorboards were creaky.

Almost directly across from the stairs was the main bathroom. There was a jacuzzi tub in here, tiles lined up about halfway and this tile was white marble instead of the blue. The bathroom was a purple and white theme. If you walked to the right of the stairs, there was a hallway closet and then three bedrooms at the end of that hallway. The bedroom on the left of that dead end was called the "back bedroom" and was just used for guests pretty much, but my dad liked to put some special memorabilia in there. The middle back room was the "playroom." In here, there was a huge wooden entertainment system that honestly hadn't moved since I could remember. It was full of various games: Sony Dreamcast, Xbox, PlayStation 2, GameCube, Nintendo 64, et cetera, and the games were encased in the middle cabinets. In the corner of this room, there was a large desk with a computer on it. The computer was something I also used in the early 2000s, one of the earliest Apple computers that came out. The last bedroom was to the right of the playroom. This room was used as an office. There was a huge L-shaped desk that took up most of the room. The counters of the desk were full of various items: papers, toy cars my dad collected, and a lot of other random things. This was the house that we were very fortunate to live in.

When I was there, we put on some movies that we would watch all the time. One of them was Flash Paradox, which was a really great cartoon of the superhero, Flash, running so fast that he went back in time to save his mother from being murdered. After he did this, it had a trickling effect on everything else in the world and was different from what Flash remembered. One big change was that Batman was actually Bruce Wayne's father, and he was a drunk because Bruce Wayne and his mother had died. It was crazy how much of an effect there would be on the world just by saving one person's life. My mom made omelets and scrambled eggs every morning. I could tell they were so happy to have me home finally. The puzzle pieces were back together where they should be.

We watched these and made some things for dinner. Everything was perfect and neither of my parents were out of it. It made me want to cry for leaving, as I missed it so much. The very last day I stayed there, my dad went out to the store and didn't come back for a while. I chose to meet him at the store to say goodbye because I had to leave to go back to Maryland so I could teach the next day and I had no idea how bad the traffic would be.

I called him on the phone, "Hey, where are you? I've gotta leave to head back so I can teach tomorrow."

"I'm at the grocery store at Big Y. Just stay for lunch, ok?"

"I can't, Dad. I'm sorry I've gotta head back before it gets too late, and I hit rush hour. I'm pulling into the store parking lot now so I can hug you goodbye, ok? I'll come back and visit soon, Dad. I love you."

I parked my car and as soon as I came out, I noticed him walking out of the store with a dozen roses in his arms. He walked up to me and gave me a huge hug, again lifting me off the ground.

"Please don't go," he said, crying. "Just stay for lunch, that's all."

I was crying, and this was so hard, but I had to leave so I could get back before traffic became worse. "Dad, I'll come back in just a few weeks. I don't want to leave either, Dad. We've been talking about me visiting more. I can."

# 30
## CLOSINGS

March, 2020. Ok, let's rewind a bit before that date… A few weeks, if not a month or so before this, there was speculation of a virus that was highly contagious and spreading across the world. It was rumored to have started in China and was quick to come here. The elderly were a heavy target first and thousands were dying at senior homes, which were being shut down. With Ebola and other sicknesses, I thought it would be solved somehow. But as more and more reports came out, things had to close.

The night before I had to be in school the next day, teachers were emailed from the county stating school would be closed for two weeks for a deep cleaning to ensure the virus was not in the school and wouldn't spread around. We would go back as soon as that deep cleaning was finished. I prepared myself for the worst the following day. I knew the kids wouldn't be able to even begin to comprehend exactly what was going on. They wouldn't have that routine of coming to school each day. But this would just be an extra vacation for everyone, right? We'll just get to stay home. I don't watch the news often, but when I opened up my phone to yahoo, I saw how many people had to wear ventilators and they had to use gift shops at certain hospitals as rooms because they were running out of places to keep all the patients.

I got a follow up email from the principal. She normally did not use her email after work hours and tried to persuade teachers not to work past their regular hours too for our own mental health, but a lot of us went on anyway.

Attention Teachers, tomorrow please have students clear their lockers completely and desk items. Have them bring all their items home with them so the janitors can do a deep cleaning of the classrooms. Do not clean up your rooms and put away decorations and other items. Just make sure any perishables are thrown in the garbage or taken home with you. We'll get through this together! We can do this!

I closed out of the email and leaned back in my seat. The first person I called was my dad.

"They're closing my school for two weeks, Dad," I said.

"Wow, really? This covid has been going around really bad."

"You should get your groceries delivered. I'll even do it for you on the computer so you're safe," I said.

"No, I got it Slim. Don't worry. So the kids are going in tomorrow and taking their stuff home with them?" he asked.

"Yeah, it's going to be a complete disaster tomorrow. No one knows what to do or what is going on and the kids are going to be even more confused than we are," I said, puzzled by how I was going to get through the next day.

"It's for everyone's safety. You've got this, Slim. Remember what I told you. You can do anything if you put your mind to it," he said back to me. We started talking about other things like when I was hopefully going to be up to visit again and then he put Mom on the phone.

"Hey, I heard they're closing your school for two weeks! That is crazy. I think they're closing schools over here, too.

"Yeah, it's going to be very hectic tomorrow, and I don't even know how to explain it to the kids. Some will be excited because they'll see it as a vacation from school, but I know the others will be upset." I went on to tell her about the google Classroom idea I had so I could still assign things to my students if they wanted to practice. She agreed with me that the closure would likely be longer.

George wanted to go visit his family for a day for his sister's birthday before it got too bad, and I just tried to map out what to do. I stayed up till around eleven or twelve that night to create a Google Classroom for my students so I could have them join it the following day before they were home for two weeks. I made one for literacy, another for math, and a third one for social studies and science. I then drafted up a letter to send home with families via email and paper copy the following day so the kids had directions on how to join in case I was not able to help them join in the next day. I just felt like it was an injustice to their education to not give them anything at all.

I don't know how I slept that night.

The next morning, I had a clear agenda in my mind. Everyone had said we would just be closed for two weeks, but in my gut I knew that wasn't going to happen. I had a feeling I wouldn't see these students again for the rest of the school year. It's just that nothing like this had ever happened before and to close an entire school down; let me rephrase that…to close down schools across the country—around the world—was a pretty damn big deal. Teachers were scrambling like crazy all about their rooms. I stood outside of my room when the bell rang to tell my students to go straight to their lockers and empty them out first thing, so that was taken care of at least. Many students hoarded a lot of things in their lockers, so this took a while. I let them come in and start putting away things in their desks. All they needed was a Chromebook. That's it. This was a half day of school, so we had limited time to do these things. When they were all packed up, I taught them how to join my Google Classroom and they thought it was the coolest thing ever. Little did they know it would soon become a norm for them and a new way of learning that had never been used across the globe.

When it was almost time to go, one of my students came to me and had said, "But Ms. D'Angelo, when will I see you again?" she asked. I gulped, as I didn't want to show my fear to her. We're supposed to have our shit together for the kids. I couldn't show that we had no idea what was going on.

"Just think of it as a long vacation. I'll see you again! Don't worry!" I said. "We'll talk on Google Classroom, too!" I reminded her, also reassuring myself in a way.

"Ok, if you say so, Ms. D'Angelo. I love you," she said. I had to turn myself away from her and thank God the lights were off in the classroom so they didn't see the tear run down my cheek. Soon after that, all the students left to go home. To go home for the rest of the year? We had no idea.

I sat down in my empty classroom and felt like a piece of my soul was ripped out. Teaching was my life, and all I knew. What would happen to these kids? I had to help them boost their reading levels and support them with math. What about seeing their friends? Recess? Lunch? What about the children that used school as their only escape from their homes? Some kids were raised in violent homes or abusive homes, too. They wouldn't be able to escape it any longer.

# 31
## TRAGEDY

In the blink of an eye, one deep breath in, just a few seconds...your entire world can change. Everything you knew or thought you knew, ceases to exist or crashes down before you. Any pieces left slip through your fingers like you're surrounded by quicksand. You're drowning; straining to pull yourself out, but being pulled further and further down.

Let me rewind to the day just prior. I was taking a lazy night which I did not do very often. I had just downloaded the SIMS game and was building a life virtually that I only wished I could have in reality. Reality was difficult though because you required luck and money which I had neither of. So there I was making friends with animated SIMS people that did not exist and building a magnificent house equipped with an in-ground pool, walkway, garden, multi-level home and all the works. As I was deep into my virtual abyss, the backlight on my phone illuminated the screen, causing me to take my eyes off of the computer for a moment. The caller ID read, "Dad." Something in me told me I had to answer this call. Of course I would have always answered, but this time felt different. It felt urgent. I paused my game for the time being and answered his call.

"Hey Slim, what's up?" he asked. He seemed more energetic than usual, and his voice was riddled with an anxious tremble.

"Oh, I'm just playing on my computer a bit. How about you, Dad?" And there he went, talking about the problems he had been having with my mother. Having read my story, you know by now that both of my parents had great difficulty with prescription medication.

"I don't know what to do anymore with me and your mom," he said. After years and years of dealing with the same side effects, my simple response was as follows:

"Call an ambulance, Dad. You can't do much more. She's got to help herself," I said, feeling like a broken record. But this was difficult because, you see, they were very co-dependent on one another. What do I mean by this? Mom would run out of her medication and then Dad would help her because he couldn't stand to see her go through the horrible withdrawals that she would go through so he would supply her with some of his medication. Then she would repay the favor if he went through all of his medication. Saying it like this sounds very simple, but there are a lot of gray areas. When there are people who are taking too much medication, often they do not remember when they have last taken medication or how much they took. They also turn desperate, to the point where they steal from each other just to satisfy that unfulfillable craving. After I said this, Dad brought up many times in the past where he had problems with my mother, and I just let him vent. I had told both of them many times to separate from one another. But it never worked. So, here I was, letting him vent. Sometimes, venting helped. Sometimes, in this unfriendly world, if there is just one person to talk to and make us feel less alone, then it makes it that much more bearable. So, there I was: that person my dad could vent to and to help him calm down.

Eventually, we got off the phone, and I got back to my game. How stupid was I? How important was this one silly game over my family? It wasn't. I felt I did what I could, but I know I could have done more. That night after was very usual. I watched some shows and then crawled into bed to sleep. The next day was Palm Sunday, but we were at the beginning of the Pandemic of Covid-19, so I would not be going back home to be with family. A blanket of darkness drew itself around me as I drifted to sleep. But not for very long. It felt like I had just closed my eyes when I felt shaking beside me. My boyfriend woke up in a sweat and explained to me he felt like he had been stabbed in the heart. He somehow went back to sleep. I lay there for a bit, refusing to check my phone because I didn't want to get distracted and I was trying to get back to sleep too. What felt like a few minutes later turned into what felt like the end of the world for me.

This time when I woke up, I did check my phone. I had many missed calls from my mom's phone as well as my dad's phone. Then there was a message from my dad. Before reading the message, I called both numbers again and again and there was no response. I finally settled for reading the message from my dad.

Hey honey it's Mommy. Daddy passed away. His heart gave out. It'll be ok; we will get through this.

I immediately lost control of myself. I pounded on George, who had been sleeping next to me. He woke up in a sweat. "What happened? What happened?"

"He's dead. My dad is dead!" I yelled through sobbing tears. At this point, the phone had fallen to the floor, and I repeatedly hit myself over and over again. My arms flailed about and I dug my nails into my skin. I was lashing out at myself. I needed to take out all the hurt on someone, and who better to take it out on than myself? The one who had abandoned my father back home and left him? The one who lost hope for him getting better? Me. George pushed my arms down, one on each side, and begged me to stop. My heart was racing, and I knew exactly what he was saying, but heard nothing. I felt as though I was underwater and in the process of drowning. I was hyperventilating and could not catch my breath. I know George had no idea what to do or even say. He had never been through a thing like this, and that was not his fault at all. What do you say or do for someone going through this? There is no making it better.

I began to feel dizzy from all the hyperventilating and flailing about, so I fell into the pillow on the bed, but immediately grew uncomfortable again. I rushed downstairs and collapsed on the couch, again starting to lash out at my own legs and arms, just digging my nails into my skin again and again. My mind instantly went to my grandparents and my mom. I had tried to call my mom repeatedly, but there was no answer. This added another worry to me because I knew she had some problems as well, so now I didn't know if I was going to be without both parents. I didn't want to call my grandparents yet because sometimes my parents hallucinated, so this could just be a bad hallucination. Yes, that's what it was. That was all. I decided to call all the nearby emergency rooms.

"Yale Emergency," the lady picked up.
It took everything in me to speak. "M-m-my dad, is he there?" I asked, feeling as though I was just four or five years old again. I felt so small and squished.
"Honey, you're going to have to give me a name. What is your dad's name?"
I gave them his name, feeling like my heart was going to burst out of my chest at any moment. The lady put me on a brief hold and then said what I feared the most:
"We don't have anyone by that name, sorry."
I hung up and dialed another emergency room. Then another. Then another. It was all the same, so I decided to call my grandparents, who lived about six or so minutes from my dad. Nonno picked up right away.
"Rissa," he said, sobbing on the other end of the phone.
"Nonno, is it true?" I asked.
"Yes, Rissa. I don't know what happened. Joey, he's gone. I'm so sorry, Rissa," Nonno said. I could hear Nonni sobbing in the background uncontrollably.
"How did it happen? I don't understand. I talked to him last night. He was just here. What happened?" I asked.
"Your mom said it was a heart attack," he said.
"She's not answering. I thought she was gone too," I said.
"She is there. She wasn't right though...I don't know, Rissa," he said, then we hung up; neither of us having the energy

to speak at all. At this point, I opened up a picture of my dad and me on my phone and just lay next to it, crying. Lying down seemed to be even worse than getting up and doing things. I felt a pain I had never felt before. No car accidents that I have been in, glass window shards falling into my back, Kawasaki Syndrome...nothing could top the pain I felt inside me. The worst part is that I could not do anything. I was restrained. I felt like the world had me handcuffed for life.

The rest of that day was a blur. I know I had packed at some point and planned to leave, but was shaking so badly that I did not trust myself driving. George had said he would come with me at first, but due to Covid-19, was unsure if he would be allowed to leave the state and come back not quarantining and being able to run his business although they did have a boating ban. That was the least of my worries at that point. I needed to get to Connecticut and at least be there for the family that I still had left.

This took me over a year to write. As soon as I picked up the pen, I would drop it and could barely function for a while. I had finally come back to this chapter and finished it the best I could. I knew I needed to share this story.

# 32
## PIECES

I hadn't written in weeks, which is unusual for me. The last entry was very traumatizing and took me over a year to finish, but I thought it to be necessary to get my story out.

I do not know how I managed to drive myself five hours back up to Connecticut so I could attend the funeral. I don't even remember driving, to be honest, but I somehow ended up there. As soon as I drove up, my mom walked slowly out to my car. She took one sight of me and looked down to the ground as she walked toward me. Her face was very pale and hair disheveled. She wore a black sweatshirt that was a few sizes too large for her and made me guess it was my father's. I couldn't park the car soon enough, so I ended up at the end of the driveway when I stopped the car and jumped out to run up the driveway toward her.

"I'm so sorry, Marissa," she said, sobbing uncontrollably. As if I hadn't been crying the entire way, I felt more tears streaming down my face. The wet drops traced down my cheeks and up and over my lips until I tasted their salty bitterness. Mom and I hugged, but pulled away after just a few moments as I tried to make sense of what happened.

I sat down on the ledge of the sidewalk where the garden had been and stared down at the gray cobblestone.

"I don't understand. He was fine when I talked to him on

Saturday." As soon as my mind couldn't process that he was gone any longer, I felt as though the world was going to open up from beneath me and swallow me whole. The tears came down again.

"Why did he have to go?" I said, gasping between each word. I was in a panicked state and kind of wished the world would just swallow me whole so the pain would end already. Every time I drove up the driveway, I was met with my father's arms and this time was different.

My mom sat next to me and cried, too. We were both in shock and disbelief.

We both moped around the house for the rest of the evening and the night...the night was the most difficult for me. I would lie in bed and toss and turn for hours and hours, wondering if he suffered when he died and cycling through all the stages of grief. I kept going from denial to bargaining over and over again. The what ifs flooded my mind. My dad's parents were still around. My Nonni and Nonno. They coordinated the wake and funeral. I am thankful I had them in that respect, because I wouldn't have known where to begin.

The next morning was the wake, and we would go directly to the cemetery. Normally, there would have been a mass. But with Covid-19, there couldn't be a mass and there was also limited capacity allowed at the wake. My mom sat to my right, and we arrived and parked, then headed in. I already felt a bit wobbly in my legs on the way in, but when I turned completely into the doorway to the room that my dad was in his casket, I had to find the closest seat to the door because I could no longer stand. I do not like to cry in front of people. But this. This was uncontrollable. They weren't just a few tears coming down bit by bit, but instead a whole stream flowed down my cheeks as I stared down at the ground. The same word echoed in my mind: "Gone. Gone. Gone. Gone. Gone. Gone."

Gone

My Nonno and Nonni sat in the front and their other two children were next to them. Eventually, I moved a little bit closer, but we had to keep our distance from one another due to Covid-19. No hugging or being close. When I needed it the most and knew they did too. Everyone was going up to pay their respects. It took me a very long time to find the strength to stand on my feet again, but I did eventually and walked over to the open casket. My dad. He lay there at peace, but in my head I knew he wasn't because there was still so much left for us to do. His right hand rested atop his other and they both lay palm-down on his torso. In his hands was a rosary intertwined within his fingers. I brought my shaky hand to my forehead, then to my chest and shoulders to make the sign of the cross because God Help Me and was thankful for the stand that I kneeled on. I touched his arm with one hand and instead of the warmth that I always got; it was ice cold. I cried and all I could whisper was "I love you, Dad, so much." I kept my head down on the casket for a while. Someone had told me to pick my head up; I guess I was getting the casket wet. I don't really think my dad would have cared about that at that point and it did not phase me in the slightest. I kept my focus down on the ground and slowly made my way back to the seat beside my mom. I could tell she was only holding herself together for me. She rubbed my back, but I moved a seat away from her because I did not want to be touched. I did not want to be hugged. I did not want to even be spoken to. Just as before, I wanted the earth below me to open and swallow me whole.

After the longest hour in my entire life, my mom and I carpooled over to the cemetery. This cemetery was the same one that my Great Nonno was buried in. My dad would be buried in a mausoleum, just as he was. He would have a military funeral. All the cars parked in a line next to where the priest would read near his casket. I just remember standing a few feet away from the casket and after the priest had read to us, members of the military shot their guns in the air and folded up the flag in a triangle as an honor to my dad. When I thought I had no tears left, they just kept coming. I didn't pay attention to what was going on at that moment. The flag was given to my father's parents, which later struck me that, as the only child of my father's—he did not have a wife—it should have been bestowed to me. But when you are going through a moment like that, nothing matters at that time.

We all touched my dad's casket before we left, and I got in my car and brought my mom back to where my dad and she were living. No one had spoken to one another or hugged or anything. It had been pouring during the wake and the sun was just starting to come out. Pieces. That is what I was left as.

# 33
## SURVIVAL

Each day after the funeral was survival. The worse times were at night because I'd be lying there with a wound within me that no band-aid could help; no medicine could cure. I was stuck. Since my dad lived in his father's house and paid rent each month, he wanted to sell the house as soon as possible, which he had every right to. It was all upsetting for everyone, and I did not want to be in that house one moment longer, either. The agreement was that I would have everything out within a month, which was going to be May 15th as the day that it was planned was April 15th, only a week after my dad left us.

Toward the end of my dad's life, he started to hoard like crazy. He would go to antique and thrift shops, just filling the house up with random things. Often, he would get things that reminded him of me. This was heartbreaking, too, because I knew how much he missed me. Figurines of the little seven dwarves, a snoopy phone, mickey mouse phone; so many random things. In each room I walked, I was devastated anew. I didn't dare to step foot into the master bedroom, where he died. Since this was during the COVID-19 pandemic, I was able to stay there and teach virtually, but still struggled to get out of bed each day. Honestly, the only reason I did get out was to teach. I needed to serve that purpose. I would wake up, soak in a bath because the shower head didn't work properly and then teach around 8 a.m. As soon as I was done teaching, I had to pack and organize everything in the entire house so it could be cleared out within a month. My dad's sister and brother would come when they could to help.

One day I had asked Mom about my dad, "Do you know how I can find Dad's friend, Paul? I tried looking online for his number, but I can't seem to find it. I know they were close." Something in my gut told me I had to find a way to reach Paul.

"I heard he worked at a place nearby," she had said. She didn't know much else. We continued packing things and left it at that.

Later that night, I was ready to get into bed when I noticed my mom wasn't inside. She had just been falling over because she had taken something, so I wanted to make sure she got into bed so she didn't hurt herself and I just honestly couldn't fall asleep knowing she could get hurt. I got out of bed and checked the back door. It was unlocked. When I opened it up, she didn't answer at first, but then I walked outside on the back porch and saw she was smoking a cigarette and falling over.

"Mom, please come in and just lie down in bed." She looked over at me and I could tell her eyes were drooping as she struggled to keep herself awake.

"I'll be right in," she said. This same interaction happened about three or four more times before I had finally flipped my lid.

"Please, Mom. I have to wake up early tomorrow to teach virtually and then pack the rest of the day. Please, just come in to bed. It's already past one in the morning," I said.

"I told you I'm comin'," she said and made no moves toward the house.

"Please don't do this. Please stop. Please, I don't know what to do," I said in hysterics. I walked in and slammed the door, stumbling over boxes until I got to the couch and just collapsed on it. She came in and fell over things in the kitchen and we screamed back and forth for a while until she flipped her lid.

"FUCK IT! FUCK IT ALL!!" she screamed as she took dishes

from the counter and smashed them on the floor. I ran upstairs crying and walked into the computer room where my dog was. The room was empty by now except for Meadow's dog bed. She didn't like to lie in it, so I crawled on top of it and went into the fetal position and cried myself to sleep.

I woke up the next day and saw Mom had made her way to the bed. I taught the entire morning and around lunchtime, there was a knock on the door. I ran downstairs and opened it up just a bit so I could see who it was. It was my dad's friend, Paul. I opened the door all the way and went out front.

"Paul!" I said as a tear streamed down from my eye. "I've been looking for you!" I could see he had his kids in the car in the driveway.

"How are you holding up? I've been meaning to come over sooner," he said. My mom came around the front at that point and said hello and stood next to me. As she stood there, I could tell that even Paul could see something wasn't right.

"I'm doing ok. I have a lot of stuff and need to figure out a place to put it because they're selling the house," I said.

"Put all your stuff in the garage and I can have some of my friends take it out so I can hold it for you. Here, let me give you my cell in case you need anything." I took out my phone and entered his number. We said goodbye and from that day on, he continued to call me to check that I was ok.

Before he left, he told me why he was there.

"All your dad said was 'Keep my baby safe,' and that's what I'm going to do. Anyone who knew your father knew that no trucks, cars, money, or anything else mattered to him as much as you did."

The following day, I woke up and had to peel myself out of bed. We had recently started virtual learning, and I had to be on by 9 a.m., which wasn't too bad, but I would wash up beforehand. People were at the door at about 8 a.m. to start ripping carpets out along with other things so they could get the house ready to sell. Before I could finish my bath in the tub, I heard knocking at the door and thought my mom would just get it. The knocking continued. Where was she? I pushed my head back into the water and got all the soap out and rushed to dry myself and get dressed. I hadn't even fully dressed, but still rushed downstairs to check out what was going on.

"Mom? Did you know someone's at the door?" I asked. There was a mumble from the other room. I ran over to the TV room and saw her sitting down on her bed, bent over so far that her head was about to crash into the floor. I went over to her and shook her.

"Are you ok?" I asked. She mumbled. She seemed to snap out of it a bit and then went to use the bathroom. I ran over to the front door where the knocking continued and let the people in.

"I'm so sorry! I was in the tub. I'll make sure I'm ready to open the door for you next time," I said as they walked inside.

I ran upstairs and got myself together so I could start teaching on my computer. I set up the computer on a stool and I sat with my back against the wall upstairs in the smallest bedroom because it was the one that wasn't a complete mess at the time and I knew they would be working downstairs. Teaching couldn't go by quick enough. I gave my students a movement break and quickly ran downstairs to check on my mom. She was in the same position she had been in earlier. I woke her up, then rushed back upstairs to finish teaching, hoping I wouldn't be too late.

As soon as teaching was done, I rushed downstairs and this time my mom was faced down in the kitchen. She was on the floor. I called 911 immediately, and they came. As soon as she heard I had called 911, she got angry, but was still very sleepy. The EMTs came in and one had asked her where she put her medication. She said she didn't take anything.

"Ma'am, I can tell that you did," the EMT told her. "We've got to take you to the ER. It's protocol.".

"No, I'm not going," she protested, slurring her words again

"It's not a choice. You can walk out with us or we will have to put you on this stretcher and take you out into the ambulance," he said.

"Hey, you did the right thing by calling us. Don't let her make you feel guilty. You need to be strong," he said. He wished me good luck and left with the ambulance.

I had tears streaming down my face. I was outside in the front as I watched the ambulance pull away and I dialed Nonno.

"Nonno, I called the ambulance," I said. "She's already left. I don't know for how long, but she was blue in the face and I thought she was dead, too."

"Ok Rissa, I'm coming over now," he said. He had dealt with my parents for years and years, long before I knew what exactly was even going on between them. While I waited for him, I decided to call her psychiatrist.

"Hello, I'd like to speak to the secretary for Dr. _____" I asked, politely but still shaky.

"One minute," the receptionist said. She came back on the phone and gave me the secretary's personal number.

I dialed it, and there was no answer, so I left a voicemail.

"Hi. My name is Marissa. I am calling on behalf of my mother and father, who both saw you. My dad just lost his life, and my mother is now on a very high dosage. I fear I am going to lose her, too. Please help me. I wanted to let you know what is going on. She should not be on this medication. I do not want to lose another person." I hung up and Nonno pulled up in the driveway.

# MARISSA D'ANGELO

# 34
## DON'T LOOK BACK

My mom had gone through a dark time, but she ended up going to get help. I knew she could not go back there to the house. I didn't want to stay there any longer than I had to, either. The first thing I did was look for a room to rent that could be a month to month for her. I found one that was in one of her favorite towns and close by to shopping centers so she could get a job to support herself. Before anything else, I boxed up all her belongings and moved them over there with the help of my friends. We didn't really talk much, but were able to send letters to one another.

Every night that I was still packing up the house, my entire body ached. I felt the whiplash in my neck that I had gotten years before in the accident I was in. I felt as if rocks were grinding up and down my back. But the worst feeling was the empty void in my heart. I called George a lot at that time. In fact, I had to push myself to wait to talk to him until the afternoon or so because I felt like I was calling him too much. I know he didn't know what to say or do, but I just needed to talk. About anything. One afternoon, my Nonno came over and started asking questions.

"Where's your guy? Didn't come to the funeral, is he calling you?" and I shook my head. But I stood up for him.

"His job is keeping him busy. And with Covid, he couldn't risk coming," I said, feeling defeated. All I wanted was for him to come here and be with me, but I knew sometimes his job was difficult in that it prevented him from leaving for long periods of times. I looked at my watch and it was after 4:00. I decided to walk away to the other room and tried to call him. After two rings, it went right to voicemail. This made me more eager and so I called him again. He had said that he was busy, but he just woke up around that time.

I walked into the other room and my friend had come over as well to help lift some of the boxes I organized. Nonno knew that there was no answer when I had called.

"I don't know, Rissa. You gotta figure out what you wanna do, and only you can make that decision," he said. That's what made this the most difficult decision yet. It truly did have to come from me. I nodded and then went over to my friend.

"Hey, thank you for coming to help. I really appreciate it. I packed some boxes upstairs in the computer room so those could be brought downstairs."

"Sure, I'll be upstairs. Let me know if you need anything else," he said and headed up. I stayed downstairs with Nonno.

"So where's your mother?" he asked.

"She's moved out," I said.

"You're very strong," Nonno replied to me. "You'll figure it out, girlfriend." He had an interesting way of speaking, that was for sure. Nick packed up the items that he could still pack. I went upstairs to check on him and he had a giant box in his hands and was making his way through the hallway upstairs. I let him come down the stairs before I headed up to check out what other things I could pack away and do. Most of the things were off the walls, but there were piles of items on the desk. I picked up two of the small frames that had been on the wall. They were both closely identical, but had one thing about them that stood out. They were clay imprints I had pressed my hand into when I was young and the mold hardened around the outline of my hand. There were two because my mom made one to give to my dad and my dad had one made to give to my mom. The one my mom had me make was a perfect handprint; so you could tell she held my hand and tried not to make any mess whatsoever of it. The one I did with my dad, you could tell he just let me put my hand on top. My mom always said the one I did with him had a lot more character and looked better, even though there were clumps of the clay on the sides of my handprint. My hands suddenly felt warm and like jelly, so I put them down in my lap and tucked my head in my hands to cry. I pictured my dad doing this with me. He'd say, "Ok, Slim, just put your hand right here," and he'd hold my small hand in his while he gently tapped the top of my hand to press into the clay and let me do the rest.

I heard my friend coming up the stairs and quickly wiped my tears with the sleeve of my dad's army sweatshirt I had been wearing.

# 35
## HOPE

The only means of communication I had with my mom was via mail. I felt like I was back in the 1800s or something, but it was something. The letters gave me hope that some things could turn out ok despite my whole world imploding on itself.

8-16-20

Hello, hope you're doing well. We just came back from lunch, and I have such a bad headache I hope will get better. If I had chicken soup, I wouldn't need the Tylenol. Anyway, I got three more weeks left after today. Today is going by slow because there aren't that many groups. I wish it was more structured on the weekends, so time went by quicker. The Godfather is on and there are only a few people watching it. I wish they put a comedy on or something. I'm glad that Meadow is doing better from the spider bite. That was so weird that it caused her to be unable to walk. Hopefully Ava is doing better, too. Boy, this year has really changed our lives forever. Like you said, usually people will have a death in their family, but not this many or traumatic as it has been for us. We'll get through it one day at a time. We had such a great group last night. There was a pastor that ran the group, and I learned a lot. We said the "Our Father" prayer at the end of the group. I was supposed to go to church today at 11 a.m. in the conference room upstairs, but no one wanted to go, and they ended up canceling it. They really should have more of a structured weekend because people are just smoking their brains out. At 3 p.m. today, we have our clean-up day, where we do intensive cleaning. Last Sunday, I had the cafeteria to clean. The time went by so quickly. At 4:15, we have a group, then go to dinner at 5:15, then at 7, we have our AA meeting.

I'll write you again soon. I can't believe how long it took you to get my letters. It's better late than never. Hang in there, things will get better.

Love Always, Mom.

8-20-20

Hello, I hope you're enjoying your time off from teaching. The blood pressure medication I started on Wednesday is making me feel weak and tired just a little bit. I spoke with the APRN and she said it's going to take some time for my body to adjust to it. Anyway, I just spoke with you yesterday and you said you're doing food delivery. Just be careful about the neighborhoods you go into. You should carry mace in your purse or always have it in your car. I'm so nervous about tonight's meeting. I'm hosting the AA meeting at 7 with Crystal, then I'm talking to the doctor and telling my story. I don't know where to begin. Oh well. I've got to face my fears. I just wish my heart wouldn't beat so fast when I'm in front of a group of people. I guess it will get better over time. I actually think it is good that grandma went into the hospital. She has missed a lot of her cancer appointments. Maybe the doctors will give her a referral to get help. Hopefully, it won't be too bad. Thank you for writing to me.

Love Always, Mom.

PS Joke of the day: I had a dream about a muffler and I woke up exhausted! Ha ha ha ha ha!

8-25-20

I hope you're doing well. I miss you very much. I only have a week and a day left. It's a little after nine on Tuesday and I just got back from snack.

You will be very proud of me because I actually told my story tonight at the 7 p.m. AA meeting. I was so nervous and couldn't stop my hands from shaking. My heart was also pounding. I faced my fear and told it anyway. I'm glad I did because I feel so much better. The conditions of being here changed so much since we were told four of the members and one lady from Detox tested positive for COVID-19. We were tested yesterday and should have the results back by Wednesday or Thursday. They already shut down Detox and aren't taking any new clients. I can't believe that Danbury is now considered a "Hot Zone." The CEO came in and said that Danbury was actually where the 1st COVID case was in Connecticut. That's pretty scary. My phone day is tomorrow and then again on Friday. Instead of seventeen clients here, some clients are leaving, so we'll be left with thirteen clients. A lot of clients are getting frustrated because of COVID, but I'm sticking it out. Well, we're all watching the movie Jumper now so I'm going to go and I'll write you again soon.

Love Always, Mom.

# 36
## CONFIDENCE

After losing my dad, I felt like my world was empty and everything I had known disintegrated into nothing. I spent a lot of my time doing things for my job. One day, I was scrolling through Facebook and saw an advertisement for Krav Maga right in Annapolis. I remembered how much my dad wanted me to join this self-defense.

Years before, Dad would do a sneak attack on me that always ended with tickling as he begged for mercy then got revenge on me with a wet willy. But then came the lesson on how to get out of certain holds.

He came from behind and said, "Ok Slim, if someone came up on you from behind you and you didn't see them coming, what would you do?" I modeled it for him and grabbed at his hands to pull them off, failing miserably. He let go.

"You're mini me," he always referred to me as this because in so many ways, we acted the same, but I'm small, much smaller compared to my dad who had done body building.

He continued, "Ok I'm gonna do it again, but this time shove your elbow into me." I did, but gently.

"There are a lot of smaller framed people who join the military in Israel since it's a requirement. They teach Krav Maga because at that point it is no longer strength that you want to be fighting with. It is technique. They have one over here. We can join."

Unfortunately, since my dad got in the accident, we never ended up joining together. Just a few months after he left us, I ended up joining. I made a promise to him I would keep, and I did just that.

On my first day in, I was a bit intimated. We were partnered up and practiced palm strikes. Right before we got with our partners, the instructor had us practice on air.

"Ok, fighting stance." I looked to my left and right and copied what everyone else was doing. We faced forward toward the instructor and had our non-dominant leg a step or two in front of the other leg. Both arms were up in front of our faces, palms facing out.

"On one, throw a palm strike with your left hand only once and bring it back to your fighting stance." She modeled it for us first.

"One!" She moved around the room. "Again, one!" We went through this several times and then she added some other combos.

"Ok, on two, you are going to lead with your non-dominant hand, pull it back, then throw another palm strike with your other hand. Ready…and…two! Ok again, two! Looking good…two!" She added three and four, which were just more palm strikes together.

Partners got tombstone pads and took turns shouting out a number while the other person threw that many palm strikes. I was so shy and barely hit the pad much at all. The instructor came around.

"You're doing great so far! Just keep your back right foot pointed each time you go for a strike so you're pushing your body forward into it, then recoil." She modeled it for me with my partner. I tried it and it felt much better that way.

After class, I felt like I was finally serving my purpose here and planned to continue coming back more and more. A few months went by and I tried to go to Krav Maga at least twice a week and practice the moves at home when I could. The next training session I went to, I noticed the woman who was my partner when I first joined.

"Hey, how is everything?" I asked.

"Good! I haven't seen you around. Guess we're going on

different days." I nodded and before we could continue talking, I heard the instructor yell.

"Ok everyone, one line!!" Today, we started our warmup which was first jogging around the room, then some sit-ups, push-ups, high knees, butt kickers, and bear crawls. This helped stretch our bodies so we could practice different techniques. After the warmup, we practiced palm strikes again because they were used frequently in combination with defensive maneuvers when getting out of chokeholds and such. I partnered up with the woman I had originally been with. She held the tombstone pad first.

"One!" she yelled. I gave it my all, and she was pushed back a step.

"Wow! You've been practicing! Two!" I smiled and gave out a two-palm strike combo at the pad. We went through combos one through four repeatedly and each time I took deep breaths and thought about everything I had lost the previous year and just let it all out on that tombstone.

At the end of the class, I was grabbing my water and bag when the woman approached me.

"Great job today in class! I couldn't believe you pushed me back," she said.

"Thank you, you too! Have a good night, and I'll see ya next time." I smiled on my way back to the car. I wasn't just doing this for my dad. It was for me, too.

I whispered on my way out, "Thank you, dad."

# MARISSA D'ANGELO

# 37

## MOVING FORWARD

Time. It's something that is very much out of our control. Even the wealthiest man in the world can't control it. I had spent each day trying to rush to do things I always wanted to do. I lost my mom's father a few months before my dad left. After the loss of my dad came my Nonni Maria and Nonno Fred. And after that, a girl that I went to high school with. This was all in about a year or so time frame. I quickly felt myself chasing time as I felt it running out. Each day, I'd wake up exhausted and push myself to do many things until the moment I fell asleep because I felt the clock ticking. I knew one thing for certain. I did not want to let my dad die in vain. He helped raise me and I needed to make sure I took care of the life he gave me.

I tried getting into things like yoga so I could calm down and feel stronger on the inside. One morning, I woke up a bit early to attend a class with my friend Jane outside on the green of the State House in Downtown Annapolis. The instructor had lavender incense burning, music playing, and we all followed her moves. This yoga was different, in a good way. It was more about meditation, and we focused on our breathing. There weren't too many strenuous moves, either. At the end, we laid on our backs and were each handed a cold, damp rag soaked in lavender essential oil. I put it on my entire face and just laid there. I thought of time again.

What was I doing here with yoga? There was so much to do

still and I'm laying here? Then I reminded myself: What's meant to be will be. There is no sense in rushing things. I got up and looked around. Everyone else was still lying down with the damp rag on their faces. I decided to lie back down for a few more minutes.

Breathe in…

Breathe out…

I thought of the group. We were all here in this moment, yet so much else was happening in the world. Somehow, we're blocking it all out for a few moments just to do something as simple as breathing. When I finally did get up, my friend Jane suggested we go check out the store nearby. I agreed. Why not? We walked there, but I didn't really see anything I wanted, so I just waited.

"Hey, we're doing Tarot Card reading in a few minutes if you want?" the shop owner suggested. I hesitated. Would my own death be read to me? I didn't really believe in these silly things, but questioned if I would focus on it too much. But it couldn't hurt.

"Yeah sure, what the hell." I walked over and paid ten dollars. The reader put up her hand in the back of the small shop to come over and sit beside her. She had big blue eyes and a perfect complexion. Her long hair had very bright strands of blonde and she wore a dress with several rings on her fingers.

"Hey, what's your name?" she asked as she set out the cards faced down.

"Marissa," I said, careful not to give her too much information.

"Hey Marissa, so I'm going to light a candle just to get some positive energy here, ok? And I want you to shuffle the deck however you want." I nodded and took the top half of the deck and put it on the bottom, then moved the cards around a bit more.

"Ok, thank you. I'm going to fan the cards out and you pick one from the beginning, one from the middle, and one from the end. The first one will be your past, the middle will be about your present, and the last card you pick will be about your future." I followed her instructions, and she kept those three cards I chose face down on the table. With the rest of the cards, she explained to me she didn't want their energy getting on the ones I chose, so she put them away. I just went along with it.

She unveiled the first card. It was an image of a woman upside down.

"Your life has been flipped upside down and a lot of changes have happened to the point where you're trying to figure out how to live in this new world," she said. I nodded and didn't comment back.

She flipped over the second card. This one was of a woman with one foot in the water and a bunch of arms doing many different things at once.

"You're trying to do too much at one time and balancing everything from your life being flipped upside down." She continued talking as she flipped the last card over.

"This last card represents the future." This one was of an incomplete tower of cups and in the distance a girl was looking out the other way with the incomplete tower behind her.

"The girl in this one is you and shows you looking to the future and moving forward. Even though the tower behind her is incomplete, she needs to leave it in the past and move on with her life. Your life has been flipped upside down. You're trying to balance too many things right now, but all you can do is move forward."

MARISSA D'ANGELO

# AFTERWARD

I am usually a writer of fiction as I've found it to be a nice escape when you can create a world straight out of your imagination and make the impossible happen. It is reassuring when you can create happy endings that you couldn't have in life, but after writing several fictional stories, I had realized something. Many of the characters that I have created are, in fact, based on people that I hold dear to my heart. The many dated letters that Chasing Time contains are real as I copied them straight from the old letter that my grandma, Martha wrote to letters my mom sent me from rehab and entries in my own personal diaries. When I started writing Chasing Time, I began with the sole purpose of wanting to be understood. I felt that the people around me never understood how grief works after losing so many people…I felt that people didn't understand that drug addicts were still people underneath their addiction. It turns out that no matter what, those people do still love you and they cannot control their addiction, which is the very sad truth of it all. I wrote Chasing Time to let you know that you are not alone in whatever you may be going through. Although I usually write fiction, I've found that some seemingly impossible things can actually happen in your reality. I never thought that I would come out of the dark hole that I felt my life became and someway…somehow, I am still going. Despite the many tragic things that have happened in my life, it is hope that I hold onto. The hope that my mother and father taught me from a young age that would allow you to accomplish and get through anything if you put your mind to it.

Thank you for reading my story.

# MARISSA D'ANGELO

www.ingramcontent.com/pod-product-compliance
Lightning Source LLC
Chambersburg PA
CBHW020237130626
46549CB00005B/1929